Splenda®
Brand

Publications International, Ltd.

Nutritional Analysis: Every effort has been made to check the accuracy of the nutritional information that appears with each recipe. However, because numerous variables account for a wide range of values for certain foods, nutritive analyses in this book should be considered approximate. Different results may be obtained by using different nutrient databases and different brand-name products.

Microwave Cooking: Microwave ovens vary in wattage. Use the cooking times as guidelines and check for doneness before adding more time.

Preparation/Cooking Times: Preparation times are based on the approximate amount of time required to assemble the recipe before cooking, baking, chilling or serving. These times include preparation steps such as measuring, chopping and mixing. The fact that some preparations and cooking can be done simultaneously is taken into account. Preparation of optional ingredients and serving suggestions is not included.

For consumer inquires, contact SPLENDA® at 1-800-777-5363.

Contents

From morning sips to midnight snacks, bring a little sweet to your day.

Celebrate just what's good in life with this collection of recipes from the SPLENDA® Kitchen. From a quick weekday morning breakfast on the go to the decadent dessert that caps off a perfect Sunday dinner, this cookbook covers it all without all of the extra added calories from sugar. So keep these delicious SPLENDA® Recipes at your fingertips, and keep your family coming back for more!

And speaking of more, enjoy the whole family of SPLENDA® Sweetener Products with your family.

- **SPLENDA® No Calorie Sweetener, Granulated**

  Cook and bake with all the sweet taste you love, and without all the added calories from sugar.

- **SPLENDA® No Calorie Sweetener, Packets**

  Sprinkle all the sweet taste without all the added calories from sugar on fresh fruit, cereal, and oatmeal, and in your beverages.

- **SPLENDA® Sugar Blend**

  Bake moist, fluffy masterpieces with half the sugar and half the calories.

- **SPLENDA® Brown Sugar Blend**

  Savor the rich taste and aroma of brown sugar, with half the sugar and half the calories.

- **SPLENDA® No Calorie Sweetener Flavors for Coffee**

  Transform your everyday cup of joe into a coffeehouse creation.

- **SPLENDA® No Calorie Sweetener Minis**

  Take the sweet taste of SPLENDA® No Calorie Sweetener with you wherever you go.

- **SPLENDA® No Calorie Sweetener Café Sticks**

  Entertain in style with these beautifully designed SPLENDA® No Calorie Sweetener sticks.

- **SPLENDA® No Calorie Sweetener with Fiber**

  Enjoy the sweet taste you love, with a little boost of fiber.

- **SPLENDA® No Calorie Sweetener FLAVOR ACCENTS™**

  Add a hint of flavor to your water without adding calories.

Quick Breads
& Breakfast Foods

Splenda Brand

Get ready for sweetness!

Banana Mini-Chip Muffins

2 cups all-purpose flour

2 teaspoons baking powder

½ teaspoon salt

¾ cup light butter, softened

⅓ cup SPLENDA® Sugar Blend

⅓ cup SPLENDA® Brown Sugar Blend, packed

1 teaspoon vanilla extract

3 medium ripe bananas, mashed

1 large egg

1 (12-ounce) package NESTLÉ® TOLL HOUSE® Semi-Sweet Chocolate Mini Morsels

1. Preheat oven to 350°F. Spray 48 mini-muffin cups with nonstick cooking spray; set aside.

2. Combine flour, baking powder, and salt in medium bowl; set aside.

3. Combine butter, SPLENDA® Sugar Blend, SPLENDA® Brown Sugar Blend, and vanilla in large bowl; beat at medium speed with a mixer until creamy. Beat in bananas and egg. Gradually mix in flour mixture; stir in morsels. Spoon batter evenly into prepared pan, filling cups two-thirds full.

4. Bake 15 to 20 minutes or until wooden pick inserted in centers comes out clean. Cool 10 minutes in pans on wire rack. Remove muffins from pans to wire rack to cool completely.

Makes 48 Servings

Nutrients per Serving:
Calories 90 (Calories from Fat 35), Protein 1g, Fat 4g (Saturated Fat 2g), Carbohydrates 13g, Fiber 0g, Cholesterol 10mg, Sodium 55mg, Sugars 8g

Apple Pie Oatmeal

1 **cup water**

½ **cup old-fashioned oats**

1 **dash salt (optional)**

Apple Pie Topping:

2 **teaspoons SPLENDA®
Brown Sugar Blend**

1 **tablespoon chopped
apple**

1 **dash apple pie spice**

1. **Stovetop Directions:** Bring water to a boil in a small saucepan. Stir in oats and salt. Cook, stirring occasionally, over medium heat 5 minutes.

   or

   Microwave Directions: Combine water, oats, and salt in a microwave-safe bowl. Cover tightly with heavy-duty plastic wrap; fold back a small edge to allow steam to escape. Microwave on high 2½ to 3 minutes; stir well.

2. Top oatmeal with SPLENDA® Brown Sugar Blend, chopped apple, and spice.

Makes 1 Serving

Nutrients per Serving:
Calories 200 (Calories from Fat 25), Protein 7g, Fat 3g (Saturated Fat 0g), Carbohydrates 37g, Fiber 5g, Cholesterol 0mg, Sodium 400mg, Sugars 10g

PREP TIME: **20 Minutes**
COOK TIME: **25 Minutes**
TOTAL TIME: **45 Minutes**

Cheery Cherry Muffins

½ **pound fresh or frozen cherries, pitted**

¼ **cup margarine**

¼ **cup reduced-fat cream cheese**

½ **cup SPLENDA® No Calorie Sweetener, Granulated**

1 **large egg**

2 **cups self-rising flour, sifted**

1 **cup nonfat milk**

1. Preheat oven to 400°F. Line a 12-cup muffin tin with paper liners. Lightly spray liners with nonstick cooking spray.

2. Set aside 12 cherries. Chop remaining cherries. Place cherries on a paper towel to drain.

3. Beat margarine and cream cheese at medium speed with an electric mixer until creamy. Add SPLENDA® Granulated Sweetener, beating well. Add egg, beating until blended.

4. Add flour to margarine mixture alternately with milk, beginning and ending with flour. Beat at low speed until blended after each addition. Do not overbeat. Stir in chopped cherries. Spoon 1 tablespoon of batter into each muffin cup. Place a cherry in the center of each cup. Top with remaining batter, filling muffin cups three-fourths full.

5. Bake in preheated oven 25 minutes or until muffins are lightly browned. Remove from pans immediately, and cool on wire racks.

Makes 12 Servings

Nutrients per Serving:
Calories 150 (Calories from Fat 50), Protein 4g, Fat 6g (Saturated Fat 1g),
Carbohydrates 21g, Fiber 1g, Cholesterol 20mg, Sodium 340mg, Sugars 5g

PREP TIME: **5 Minutes**
TOTAL TIME: **5 Minutes**

Berry Simple Smoothie

- **2 cups frozen unsweetened whole strawberries**
- **1 cup plain nonfat yogurt**
- **½ cup lite cranberry juice**
- **¼ cup SPLENDA® No Calorie Sweetener, Granulated**

Combine frozen strawberries, yogurt, cranberry juice, and SPLENDA® Granulated Sweetener in a blender until smooth, stopping to scrape down sides.

Makes 3 Servings

Nutrients per Serving:
Calories 110 (Calories from Fat 0), Protein 5g, Fat 0g (Saturated Fat 0g), Carbohydrates 22g, Fiber 3g, Cholesterol 0mg, Sodium 65mg, Sugars 18g

Oat Bran Pancakes

1 cup oat bran hot cereal, uncooked

½ cup all-purpose flour

¼ cup SPLENDA® No Calorie Sweetener, Granulated

1 teaspoon baking powder

½ teaspoon baking soda

⅛ teaspoon salt

2 cups buttermilk

¼ cup egg substitute

1. Heat nonstick griddle or frying pan over medium to medium high heat.

2. Combine oat bran, flour, SPLENDA® Granulated Sweetener, baking powder, baking soda, and salt in a large bowl. Set aside.

3. Beat together buttermilk and egg substitute in a small bowl with a wire whisk. Pour the egg mixture over dry ingredients. Stir together until ingredients are just blended and no large dry lumps appear.

4. Pour approximately ¼ cup pancake batter onto hot griddle. Cook pancakes until puffed, browned, and slightly dry around the edges. Flip over and cook other side until golden brown.

Makes 6 Servings

Nutrients per Serving:
Calories 130 (Calories from Fat 20), Protein 7g, Fat 2g (Saturated Fat 1g), Carbohydrates 20g, Fiber 2g, Cholesterol 5mg, Sodium 300mg, Sugars 4g

Crispy French Toast

1 cup 1% low-fat milk

¾ cup half and half

½ cup SPLENDA®
No Calorie Sweetener,
Granulated

2 tablespoons vanilla
extract

4 large eggs

6 thick slices white
bread, crusts removed
and cut diagonally in
half

4 cups cornflakes cereal,
finely crushed

2 tablespoons ground
cinnamon

1 cup strawberries, sliced

1 cup fat-free vanilla
yogurt

Optional Garnish: fresh
mint sprigs

1. Preheat oven to 350°F.

2. Combine milk, half and half, SPLENDA® Granulated Sweetener, and vanilla; whisk until SPLENDA® Granulated Sweetener dissolves. Add eggs, whisking until blended.

3. Dip bread into the milk mixture; dredge in cornflakes cereal. Place on a baking sheet.

4. Bake for 5 to 10 minutes or until golden brown.

5. Sprinkle a small amount of cinnamon over 6 plates. Arrange 2 toast triangles in the center of each plate. Arrange strawberries around toast; top toast with a small scoop of vanilla yogurt. Sprinkle with cinnamon. Garnish with fresh mint sprigs, if desired.

Makes 6 Servings

Nutrients per Serving:
Calories 320 (Calories from Fat 80), Protein 12g, Fat 9g (Saturated Fat 4g), Carbohydrates 44g, Fiber 3g, Cholesterol 155mg, Sodium 460mg, Sugars 10g

Lemon Poppy Seed Muffins

2¼ **cups cake flour**

¾ **cup SPLENDA®
No Calorie Sweetener,
Granulated**

¼ **cup sugar**

¾ **cup unsalted butter,
softened**

½ **cup nonfat dry milk**

2 **teaspoons baking
powder**

¾ **teaspoon baking soda**

¼ **teaspoon salt**

¾ **cup buttermilk**

2 **tablespoons lemon
juice**

2 **tablespoons grated
lemon peel**

3 **eggs**

2 **teaspoons vanilla
extract**

2 **tablespoons poppy
seeds**

1. Preheat oven to 350°F. Line an 18-cup muffin tin with paper liners. Set aside.

2. Place cake flour, SPLENDA® Granulated Sweetener, sugar, and softened butter in a large mixing bowl. Mix on medium speed 1 to 2 minutes with an electric mixer until the butter is mixed into the flour mixture, with only very small pieces of butter visible.

3. Add nonfat dry milk, baking powder, baking soda, and salt. Mix on low speed until blended.

4. Mix buttermilk, lemon juice, lemon peel, eggs, and vanilla in a small bowl. Stir well. Add ⅔ of the buttermilk mixture to the flour mixture. Mix on medium speed mixing until the liquids are just blended into the flour mixture. Stop the mixer and scrape the sides and bottom of the bowl. Mix on medium-high speed about 45 to 60 seconds until the batter starts to get lighter in appearance. Reduce mixer speed to low and add remaining liquids. Mix on medium speed until blended. Stop mixer and scrape sides and bottom of bowl again. Add poppy seeds. Mix on medium high speed an additional 30 seconds.

5. Pour muffin batter into prepared pans. Bake muffins in preheated oven 12 to 15 minutes or until a wooden toothpick inserted in the center of the cupcake comes out clean.

Makes 18 Servings

Breakfast Trifle

**½ cup SPLENDA®
No Calorie Sweetener,
Granulated**

**4 cups plain nonfat
yogurt**

**2 teaspoons vanilla
extract**

**9 slices Italian-style or
other white bread,
crusts removed**

**12 ounces frozen
unsweetened
raspberries, thawed**

**2 tablespoons SPLENDA®
No Calorie Sweetener,
Granulated**

**1 (15-ounce) can cling
peaches, no sugar
added, drained**

**16 ounces frozen dark
pitted sweet cherries,
thawed and drained**

1 banana, thinly sliced

1. Blend ½ cup of SPLENDA® Granulated Sweetener, yogurt, and vanilla together in a medium mixing bowl. Set aside.

2. Cut bread into rectangles.

3. Mix together raspberries and 2 tablespoons SPLENDA® Granulated Sweetener gently. Do not drain raspberries.

4. To assemble trifle: Pour ½ cup of yogurt mixture in the bottom of the glass bowl.

5. Place ⅓ of the sliced bread on top of the yogurt mixture. Top bread with ⅓ of the peaches, ⅓ of the cherries and ⅓ of the raspberries. Drizzle about ⅓ of the raspberry juice onto the bread. Place ⅓ of the thinly sliced banana on top of the raspberries. Pour ⅓ of the yogurt mixture over the bread and fruit.

6. Repeat step 5 two more times, ending by pouring the remaining yogurt over the fruit.

7. Cover and refrigerate at least 2 hours or overnight, allowing the bread to fully absorb the fruit juices.

Makes 10 Servings

Nutrients per Serving:
Calories 200 (Calories from Fat 10), Protein 8g, Fat 1g (Saturated Fat 0g),
Carbohydrates 39g, Fiber 3g, Cholesterol 0mg, Sodium 190mg, Sugars 17g

PREP TIME: **15 Minutes**
COOK TIME: **50 Minutes**
TOTAL TIME: **9 Hours**

French Toast Strata

⅓ cup SPLENDA®
No Calorie Sweetener,
Granulated

1 cup egg substitute

⅔ cup nonfat milk

¾ teaspoon imitation
maple flavor

8 slices cinnamon-raisin
bread

2 cups peeled apples,
thinly sliced

¼ cup low-fat cream
cheese

1 tablespoon SPLENDA®
No Calorie Sweetener,
Granulated

½ teaspoon ground
cinnamon

1. Preheat oven to 350°F. Spray an 8×8-inch square cake pan with nonstick cooking spray. Set aside.

2. Blend together ⅓ cup SPLENDA® Granulated Sweetener, egg substitute, milk, and maple flavor in a medium bowl.

3. Tear cinnamon raisin bread into pieces, approximately 1 to 2 inches each. Add bread and sliced apples into mixing bowl with other ingredients. Toss to coat bread. Pour bread mixture into prepared pan.

4. Cut cream cheese into 8 chunks and place on top of strata.

5. Blend remaining 1 tablespoon SPLENDA® Granulated Sweetener and cinnamon together. Sprinkle over strata. Cover and refrigerate overnight.

6. Bake in a preheated oven 40 to 50 minutes or until lightly browned and set. Serve immediately.

Makes 8 Servings

Nutrients per Serving:
Calories 150 (Calories from Fat 35), Protein 8g, Fat 4g (Saturated Fat 1g),
Carbohydrates 21g, Fiber 2g, Cholesterol 5mg, Sodium 200mg, Sugars 11g

Strawberry Orange Smash Smoothie

3 cups frozen strawberries, unsweetened

⅔ cup SPLENDA® No Calorie Sweetener, Granulated

1¼ cups orange juice, calcium fortified

1 cup plain nonfat yogurt

½ teaspoon vanilla extract

¼ cup ice cubes

Add all ingredients to blender. Blender will be full. Mix on low speed for 10 seconds. Remove lid, stir with wooden spoon. Mix on medium speed for 15 to 20 seconds; remove lid and stir again. Mix on high speed for 15 to 20 seconds or until smooth. Pour into glasses. Serve immediately.

Makes 5 Servings

Nutrients per Serving:
Calories 80 (Calories from Fat 0), Protein 3g, Fat 0g (Saturated Fat 0g), Carbohydrates 19g, Fiber 2g, Cholesterol 0mg, Sodium 30mg, Sugars 14g

Pumpkin Waffles

- 1 **cup all-purpose flour**
- 1 **teaspoon baking powder**
- ½ **teaspoon baking soda**
- ¼ **teaspoon salt**
- ¾ **teaspoon ground cinnamon**
- ½ **teaspoon ground ginger**
- ⅛ **teaspoon ground nutmeg**
- 2 **teaspoons canola oil**
- 1 **teaspoon molasses**
- ¼ **cup canned pumpkin**
- 1 **cup buttermilk**
- 1 **large egg**
- 2 **tablespoons SPLENDA® No Calorie Sweetener, Granulated**
- 1½ **cups maple syrup sweetened with SPLENDA® Brand Sweetener**

1. Preheat waffle iron according to manufacturer's directions; spray lightly with nonstick cooking spray.

2. Combine flour, baking powder, soda, salt, cinnamon, ginger, and nutmeg in a large bowl. Set aside.

3. Combine oil, molasses, pumpkin, and buttermilk in a small bowl; set aside.

4. Whisk together egg and SPLENDA® Granulated Sweetener until blended. Add buttermilk mixture, whisking until blended. Add to dry ingredients, stirring just until moistened.

5. Pour batter into a hot waffle iron and bake approximately 5 minutes. Serve with maple syrup.

Makes 6 Servings

Nutrients per Serving:
Calories 160 (Calories from Fat 25), Protein 5g, Fat 3g (Saturated Fat 1g), Carbohydrates 32g, Fiber 1g, Cholesterol 35mg, Sodium 400mg, Sugars 3g

PREP TIME: **20 Minutes**
COOK TIME: **20 Minutes**
TOTAL TIME: **40 Minutes**

German Apple Pancakes

1 **tablespoon ground cinnamon**

1 **tablespoon sugar**

½ **cup all-purpose flour**

1 **tablespoon baking powder**

½ **teaspoon baking soda**

3 **tart apples**

4 **large eggs**

½ **cup 2% reduced-fat milk**

1 **cup SPLENDA® No Calorie Sweetener, Granulated**

3 **egg whites**

4 **tablespoons butter**

1. Preheat oven to 350°F.

2. Mix cinnamon and sugar together; set aside.

3. Sift together flour, baking powder, and baking soda; set aside.

4. Peel, core, and slice the apples.

5. Combine whole eggs, milk, and SPLENDA® Granulated Sweetener in a food processor.

6. Whip egg whites in a separate bowl to soft peaks. Gently fold egg whites into egg mixture. Add flour mixture into the batter and gently fold until well mixed.

7. Melt 1 tablespoon butter over medium heat in a medium-sized, oven-proof frying pan. Add one-fourth of the apples and ½ tablespoon cinnamon-sugar mixture. Cook until apples begin to brown. Pour one-fourth of the pancake batter into the pan.

8. Place pan in the preheated oven and bake 12 to 15 minutes or until firm.

9. Remove pancake from pan by turning upside down onto a plate.

10. Repeat with remaining batter.

11. Garnish with fresh fruit or crème fraîche, if desired.

12. Serve immediately.

Makes 8 Servings

Nutrients per Serving:
Calories 180 (Calories from Fat 80), Protein 6g, Fat 9g (Saturated Fat 5g), Carbohydrates 20g, Fiber 2g, Cholesterol 125mg, Sodium 280mg, Sugars 11g

Miniature Apple Muffins

¾ **cup SPLENDA®
No Calorie Sweetener,
Granulated**

1 **cup butter, softened**

2 **teaspoons molasses**

2 **large eggs**

⅓ **cup apple juice
concentrate, thawed**

2 **teaspoons grated fresh
lemon peel**

2 **cups all-purpose flour**

2 **teaspoons ground
cinnamon**

1 **teaspoon ground
nutmeg**

1 **teaspoon baking soda**

½ **teaspoon salt**

1 **cup peeled, shredded
fresh apple**

⅔ **cup old-fashioned oats**

½ **cup raisins**

1. Preheat oven to 400°F. Lightly spray mini-muffin cups with nonstick cooking spray; set aside.

2. Beat SPLENDA® Granulated Sweetener, butter, and molasses at medium speed of an electric mixer 1 minute or until blended. Add eggs, one at a time, beating until blended after each addition; add apple juice concentrate and lemon peel, beating until blended.

3. Combine flour, cinnamon, nutmeg, soda, and salt; add to SPLENDA® Granulated Sweetener mixture, beating on low speed just until blended. Stir in apple, oats, and raisins.

4. Spoon batter into prepared pans; filling three-fourths full. Bake until edges are lightly browned, 12 minutes. Remove to wire racks to cool.

Makes 36 Servings

Nutrients per Serving:
Calories 100 (Calories from Fat 50), Protein 1g, Fat 6g (Saturated Fat 3g),
Carbohydrates 11g, Fiber 1g, Cholesterol 25mg, Sodium 125mg, Sugars 4g

Banana Rolls

¾ **cup SPLENDA®
No Calorie Sweetener,
Granulated**

1 **(8-ounce) package
⅓-less-fat cream
cheese**

2 **bananas**

2 **teaspoons vanilla
extract**

2 **(10-ounce) cans
reduced-fat crescent
rolls**

1. Preheat oven to 350°F.

2. Mix SPLENDA® Granulated Sweetener, cream
   cheese, bananas, and vanilla in a medium
   mixing bowl using a hand mixer. Mix until
   creamy.

3. Place crescent rolls on an ungreased baking
   sheet. Spread about 1 tablespoon of filling
   onto each crescent roll and roll into crescent
   shape.

4. Bake in preheated oven 12 to 15 minutes or
   until lightly browned.

Makes 16 Servings

Nutrients per Serving:
Calories 180 (Calories from Fat 70), Protein 4g, Fat 8g (Saturated Fat 3g),
Carbohydrates 21g, Fiber 0g, Cholesterol 5mg, Sodium 360mg, Sugars 8g

Pineapple Plantain Muffins

1 large ripe plantain

¼ teaspoon light butter

1½ teaspoons ground cinnamon

2 cups all-purpose flour plus 2 tablespoons all-purpose flour

2 teaspoons baking powder

½ teaspoon baking soda

2 tablespoons light butter

¾ cup SPLENDA® Sugar Blend

⅓ cup SPLENDA® Brown Sugar Blend

2 egg whites

1 egg yolk

8 ounces light vanilla yogurt

1 teaspoon vanilla extract

1 small ripe banana, mashed

¾ cup pineapple chunks

½ cup sliced almonds, for garnish (optional)

1. **Prepare plantain:** Preheat oven to 350°F. Slice skin of plantain and spread butter and cinnamon on top. Wrap in aluminum foil and bake for 45 minutes. Allow to cool. Remove from skin and set aside.

2. **Prepare muffins:** Sift flour, baking powder, and baking soda into a small bowl. In a large bowl, cream butter, SPLENDA® Sugar Blend, and SPLENDA® Brown Sugar Blend. Add egg whites and yolk, yogurt, vanilla, banana, and plantain.

3. Fold in flour mixture and pineapple.

4. Line muffin pans with paper liners. Fill each liner about two-thirds full with batter. Top with sliced almonds, if desired.

5. Bake in preheated oven 18 to 22 minutes or until a toothpick inserted in the center comes out clean.

Makes 15 Servings

Nutrients per Serving:
Calories 210 (Calories from Fat 30), Protein 4g, Fat 3g (Saturated Fat 1g), Carbohydrates 38g, Fiber 1g, Cholesterol 20mg, Sodium 135mg, Sugars 20g

Caramel Sticky Buns

Rolls:

- 1 cup water
- ¼ cup butter
- 1 (.25-ounce) envelope active dry yeast
- ½ cup warm water (100°F. to 110°F.)
- 2 large eggs
- ¼ cup SPLENDA® Sugar Blend
- 1¼ teaspoons salt
- 5 cups all-purpose flour
- 1 cup chopped pecans
- ¼ cup butter, melted
- 1 cup SPLENDA® Brown Sugar Blend
- 1 teaspoon ground cinnamon

Caramel Sauce:

- ⅓ cup butter
- 3 tablespoons 2% reduced-fat milk

- 2 tablespoons light corn syrup
- ¾ cup SPLENDA® Brown Sugar Blend

1. Bring water to a boil in a small saucepan; remove from heat and add butter, stirring until butter melts. Let stand until mixture cools (about 20 minutes).

2. Combine yeast and warm water in a glass measuring cup; let mixture stand 5 minutes.

3. Beat eggs at medium speed using a heavy-duty stand mixer; add SPLENDA® Sugar Blend and salt, beating until blended. Add yeast mixture and butter mixture, beating on low speed until blended. Gradually add flour, beating until blended.

4. Turn dough out onto a well-floured surface and knead until smooth and elastic (about 5 minutes). Place in a well greased bowl, turning to grease top. Cover and chill dough 8 hours or up to 3 days.

5. **Prepare Caramel Sauce:** Immediately pour into 3 lightly greased 8-inch round or square cake pans. Sprinkle each pan with ⅓ cup pecans.

6. Punch dough down and divide into 3 equal portions. Roll one portion of dough into a 12×10-inch rectangle. Brush with melted butter.

7. Combine SPLENDA® Brown Sugar Blend and cinnamon; sprinkle ⅓ cup mixture over

Nutrients per Serving:
Calories 260 (Calories from Fat 100), Protein 3g, Fat 11g (Saturated Fat 5g), Carbohydrates 34g, Fiber 1g, Cholesterol 35mg, Sodium 190mg, Sugars 16g

each rectangle. Roll up starting at long edge; pinch edges to seal. Cut log into 9 slices. Arrange slices cut-side down over Caramel Sauce in pans. Repeat procedure with remaining dough.

8. Cover and let rise in a warm place (85°F.), free from drafts, 30 minutes or until doubled in bulk.

9. Preheat oven to 375°F.

0. Bake in preheated oven 20 minutes or until golden. Cool on a wire rack 5 minutes. Invert onto serving plate.

Caramel Sauce Directions: Combine butter, milk, corn syrup, and SPLENDA® Brown Sugar Blend in a small saucepan. Cook over low heat, stirring constantly until SPLENDA® Brown Sugar Blend dissolves. Bring mixture to a boil over medium-high heat; boil 1 minute.

Makes 27 Servings

Lemon-Orange Walnut Bread

- 2 **cups all-purpose flour**
- 1 **teaspoon baking powder**
- ½ **teaspoon baking soda**
- ⅔ **cup 1% low-fat milk**
- 2 **tablespoons lemon juice**
- 1½ **teaspoons freshly grated lemon peel**
- 1½ **teaspoons freshly grated orange peel**
- 2 **large eggs**
- ¾ **cup SPLENDA® No Calorie Sweetener, Granulated**
- ½ **cup butter, melted**
- 2 **teaspoons vanilla extract**
- ¾ **cup chopped walnuts**

1. Preheat oven to 350°F. Lightly spray an 8½×4½×2½-inch loaf pan with nonstick cooking spray.
2. Combine flour, baking powder, and baking soda; set aside.
3. Combine milk, lemon juice, lemon and orange peel; set aside.
4. Beat eggs and SPLENDA® Granulated Sweetener on high speed with an electric mixer for 5 minutes. Reduce speed to medium; gradually add melted butter and vanilla, beating until blended, about 1 minute.
5. Add flour mixture alternately with milk mixture; beginning and ending with flour mixture. Beat at low speed until blended after each addition. Stir in walnuts. Spoon batter into prepared loaf pan.
6. Bake in preheated oven 30 to 35 minutes or until a long wooden pick inserted in center comes out clean. Cool in pan on a wire rack 10 minutes; remove from pan and cool completely.

Makes 12 Servings

Nutrients per Serving:
Calories 220 (Calories from Fat 120), Protein 5g, Fat 14g (Saturated Fat 6g), Carbohydrates 20g, Fiber 1g, Cholesterol 55mg, Sodium 190mg, Sugars 3g

Cinnamon-Pecan Monkey Bread

¼ **cup chopped pecans**

2 **tablespoons butter**

¼ **cup SPLENDA®
Brown Sugar Blend**

¼ **teaspoon ground
cinnamon**

⅓ **cup SPLENDA®
Brown Sugar Blend**

¼ **teaspoon ground
cinnamon**

½ **(3-pound) package
frozen roll dough,
thawed**

3 **tablespoons butter,
melted**

1. Spray a 12-cup bundt pan with nonstick cooking spray. Sprinkle pecans in bottom of pan; set aside.

2. Combine 2 tablespoons butter, ¼ cup SPLENDA® Brown Sugar Blend, and ¼ teaspoon cinnamon in a small saucepan; cook over low heat, stirring constantly until blended; pour mixture over pecans. Set aside.

3. Combine ⅓ cup SPLENDA® Brown Sugar Blend and ¼ teaspoon cinnamon in a small bowl; set aside.

4. Cut each roll into half; dip tops of balls into melted butter and then into SPLENDA® Brown Sugar Blend mixture. Place in prepared pan. (At this point Monkey Bread may be covered and stored in the refrigerator 8 hours or overnight or proceed as directed). Cover and let rise in a warm place, free from drafts, 50 minutes or until doubled in bulk.

5. Preheat oven to 350°F. about 10 minutes prior to baking. Bake 25 to 30 minutes or until bread sounds hollow when tapped. Remove from pan; cool on a wire rack. Serve warm.

Makes 18 Servings

Nutrients per Serving:
Calories 180 (Calories from Fat 60), Protein 4g, Fat 6g (Saturated Fat 2g), Carbohydrates 24g, Fiber 1g, Cholesterol 10mg, Sodium 290mg, Sugars 9g

Mango Yogurt Smoothie

- **1 cup ice cubes**
- **1 large ripe mango, peeled and chopped**
- **¼ cup SPLENDA® No Calorie Sweetener, Granulated**
- **1 cup plain nonfat yogurt**
- **½ cup mango nectar or orange juice**
- **½ teaspoon almond extract**
- **Pinch of salt**

Combine all ingredients in a blender in the order listed; process mixture until smooth, stopping to scrape down sides.

Makes 3 Servings

Nutrients per Serving:
Calories 110 (Calories from Fat 0), Protein 4g, Fat 0g (Saturated Fat 0g), Carbohydrates 26g, Fiber 2g, Cholesterol 0mg, Sodium 180mg, Sugars 22g

Tasty Appetizers, Meals & Sides

Splenda Brand

Get ready for love at first sprinkle.

Easy Lemon Chicken

- 1 **teaspoon cornstarch**
- 1 **tablespoon low-sodium soy sauce**
- 12 **ounces chicken breast tenders, cut into thirds**
- ¼ **cup fresh lemon juice**
- ¼ **cup low-sodium soy sauce**
- ¼ **cup fat-free chicken broth**
- 1 **teaspoon fresh ginger, minced**
- 2 **cloves garlic, minced**
- 1 **tablespoon SPLENDA® No Calorie Sweetener, Granulated**
- 1 **teaspoon cornstarch**
- 1 **tablespoon vegetable oil**
- ¼ **cup red bell pepper, sliced into 2-inch strips**
- ¼ **cup green bell pepper, sliced into 2-inch strips**

1. Mix 1 teaspoon cornstarch and 1 tablespoon soy sauce in a small mixing bowl. Add sliced chicken tenders. Place in refrigerator and marinate for 10 minutes.

2. Stir the lemon juice, ¼ cup soy sauce, chicken broth, ginger, garlic, SPLENDA® Granulated Sweetener, and 1 teaspoon cornstarch together in a medium-sized mixing bowl.

3. Heat oil in a medium frying pan. Add chicken and cook over medium-high heat 3 to 4 minutes or until just done. Add sauce and sliced peppers. Cook 1 to 2 minutes more or until sauce thickens and peppers are slightly tender.

Makes 4 Servings

Nutrients per Serving:
Calories 150 (Calories from Fat 40), Protein 21g, Fat 5g (Saturated Fat 1g), Carbohydrates 6g, Fiber 1g, Cholesterol 50mg, Sodium 730mg, Sugars 1g

Shrimp and Corn Salad with Basil

- 2 **tablespoons olive oil**
- 4 **cups fresh corn kernels**
- ¾ **cup minced red onion**
- 2 **cups cherry tomatoes, halved**
- 4 **tablespoons olive oil**
- 6 **tablespoons lime juice**
- 4 **tablespoons SPLENDA® No Calorie Sweetener, Granulated**
- 2 **teaspoons kosher salt**
- 3 **tablespoons fresh basil leaves, cut into thin strips**
- 24 **large shrimp, peeled and deveined**
- 1 **tablespoon olive oil**
- 2 **teaspoons red pepper flakes**
- ½ **teaspoon kosher salt**
- ¼ **teaspoon black pepper**

1. Heat the oil in a medium skillet; sauté corn and red onions until tender.
2. Transfer corn mixture to a stainless bowl and add cut tomatoes. Set aside.
3. Mix olive oil, lime juice, SPLENDA® Granulated Sweetener, salt, and basil in a small stainless bowl; toss with corn.
4. Toss the shrimp, oil, red pepper flakes, salt, and pepper in a small bowl.
5. Cook shrimp on an open face grill for 2 minutes on one side and turn over for an additional minute. Place cooked shrimps into corn salad mixture.
6. Adjust seasoning and serve.

Makes 6 Servings

Nutrients per Serving:
Calories 350 (Calories from Fat 170), Protein 21g, Fat 19g (Saturated Fat 3g), Carbohydrates 27g, Fiber 4g, Cholesterol 130mg, Sodium 930mg, Sugars 9g

Cucumber and Onion Salad

2½ **cups thinly sliced
unpeeled cucumbers**

½ **cup sliced red onions**

⅓ **cup SPLENDA®
No Calorie Sweetener,
Granulated**

⅓ **cup white vinegar**

¼ **teaspoon salt**

⅛ **teaspoon black pepper**

1. Place cucumbers and onions in a non-metallic medium bowl.

2. Combine remaining ingredients in a small mixing bowl. Stir well. Pour over cucumbers and onions. Cover and refrigerate for at least 2 hours. Stir occasionally.

Makes 6 Servings

Nutrients per Serving:
Calories 15 (Calories from Fat 0), Protein 1g, Fat 0g (Saturated Fat 0g),
Carbohydrates 3g, Fiber 1g, Cholesterol 0mg, Sodium 100mg, Sugars 2g

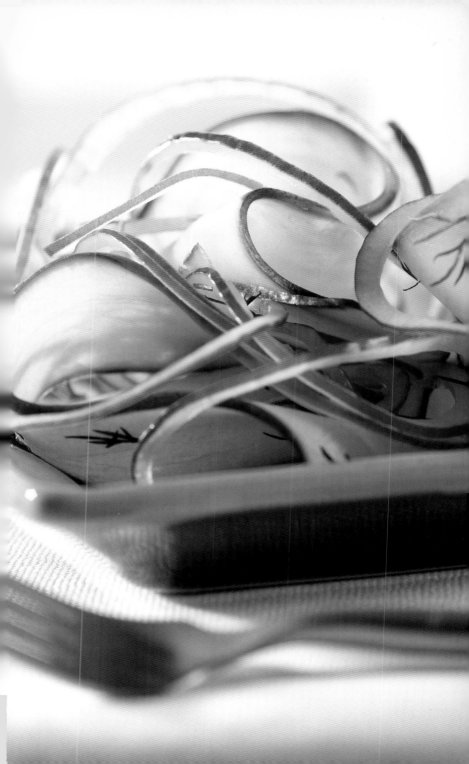

Hot German Potato Salad

- 1½ **pounds new potatoes**
- 8 **slices lean turkey bacon**
- 1 **tablespoon canola oil**
- ½ **cup diced yellow onion**
- 3 **tablespoons SPLENDA® No Calorie Sweetener, Granulated**
- 1 **teaspoon all-purpose flour**
- ¼ **teaspoon salt**
- ½ **cup water**
- ⅓ **cup white vinegar**
- 2 **tablespoons chopped parsley**

1. Wash and quarter potatoes. Place in a large pot filled with lightly salted water. Bring water to a boil and boil potatoes 15 to 20 minutes or until tender when pierced with a fork. Drain and set aside.

2. Chop bacon into strips. Place oil in a large skillet. Heat over medium-high heat. Add bacon and cook until lightly browned. Add onion and cook approximately 5 more minutes or until onions are translucent.

3. Mix SPLENDA® Granulated Sweetener, flour, and salt together in a small bowl. Stir into pan and cook briefly (approximately 1 minute). Add water and vinegar while stirring constantly. Add potatoes and stir well.

4. Garnish with chopped parsley. Serve immediately.

Makes 8 Servings

Nutrients per Serving:
Calories 110 (Calories from Fat 35), Protein 3g, Fat 4g (Saturated Fat 1g), Carbohydrates 17g, Fiber 2g, Cholesterol 10mg, Sodium 200mg, Sugars 1g

PREP TIME: **25 Minutes**
COOK TIME: **1 Hour**
TOTAL TIME: **1 Hour, 25 Minutes**

Huitlacoche (Mexican Mushrooms) Quesadilla

Filling:

- 1 medium white onion, finely chopped
- 1 tablespoon olive oil
- 1 tablespoon butter or margarine
- 1 tablespoon finely chopped garlic
- ½ pound mushrooms (field and shitake)
- 1 (7-ounce) can huitlacoche
- 1 cup SPLENDA® No Calorie Sweetener, Granulated
- 1 cup fresh corn kernels
- 1 teaspoon salt
- 1 teaspoon black pepper
- 3 tablespoons fresh parsley
- 3 tablespoons fresh cilantro

Masa*:

- 3 cups masa-harina for tortillas
- ¾ teaspoon salt
- 1¾ cups warm water

- 1 (12-ounce) container cottage cheese

1. **Prepare Filling:** In an 8-inch cast-iron frying pan, cook onion in oil and butter 5 minutes over medium heat. Add garlic and cook 3 minutes. Add mushrooms and huitlacoche and continue cooking 7 minutes. Add SPLENDA® Granulated Sweetener and corn and cook another 10 minutes.

2. Stir in salt, pepper, parsley, and cilantro. Set aside.

3. **Prepare Masa:** Heat a 10-inch comal (griddle or cast-iron frying pan) over medium heat.

4. Mix masa-harina with salt and water to make soft but not dry dough. Divide the dough into 20 balls; shape each ball into a 5-inch-long by 1½-inches-wide log.

5. Place a log between two sheets of plastic, put it in a tortilla press and press down. If you do not have a tortilla press, press with your hand and create an oval shape, turn it and press on the other side.

Nutrients per Serving:
Calories 220 (Calories from Fat 50), Protein 9g, Fat 6g (Saturated Fat 2g), Carbohydrates 34g, Fiber 6g, Cholesterol 5mg, Sodium 570mg, Sugars 4g

Remove the plastic and place over the preheated griddle. Cook for 2 to 3 minutes on each side or until it starts to brown and removes easily from the griddle without breaking.

Top each tortilla with the filling and cheese, fold and serve.

*Pre-made corn tortillas can also be warmed and filled in place of the fresh masa recipe.

Makes 10 Servings

Homemade Risotto Topped with Caramelized Apricots

Risotto:

- 1 **tablespoon olive oil**
- 1 **tablespoon minced garlic**
- 1 **tablespoon minced shallots**
- 1 **cup Arborio rice***
- 3 **cups chicken broth**
- 1 **cup freshly grated Parmigiano-Reggiano cheese**
- 1 **tablespoon butter**

Caramelized Apricots:

- 1 **cup diced fresh apricots**
- ¼ **cup water**
- 3 **tablespoons SPLENDA® Sugar Blend**
- 1 **tablespoon fresh lemon juice**
- 1 **tablespoon butter**
- ½ **cup walnut halves**

Fresh basil for garnish, optional

Freshly grated Parmigiano-Reggiano cheese for garnish, optional

1. **Prepare Risotto:** Heat olive oil in a medium saucepan over medium heat; add garlic and shallots. Cook, stirring constantly, for 3 minutes or until shallots are translucent.

2. Stir in rice and chicken broth; bring to a boil. Reduce heat to low; simmer covered 20 to 22 minutes (stirring occasionally) or until rice is tender but still firm to the bite. Remove from heat; stir in cheese and butter.

3. **Prepare Apricots:** Combine apricots, water, SPLENDA® Sugar Blend, and lemon juice in a small saucepan; bring to a boil over high heat. Stir in the butter and cook, uncovered, 5 minutes or until apricots are softened and the juices begin to brown.

4. Divide risotto among 8 shallow serving bowls; top evenly with apricots and walnuts. Garnish with basil and cheese, if desired.

---

*Arborio is a variety of Italian rice that gives risotto its creamy texture. If it is unavailable, use any short-grain rice.

Makes 8 Servings

Nutrients per Serving:
Calories 310 (Calories from Fat 140), Protein 11g, Fat 15g (Saturated Fat 6g), Carbohydrates 30g, Fiber 1g, Cholesterol 20mg, Sodium 710mg, Sugars 7g

Stir-Fried Green Beans

Stir-Fry Sauce:

- 1½ tablespoons minced garlic
- 1½ tablespoons minced fresh ginger
- 2 scallions (white and green parts), minced
- 2 tablespoons dry sherry*
- 2 tablespoons SPLENDA® No Calorie Sweetener, Granulated
- 2 tablespoons soy sauce
- 1 tablespoon water

Stir-Fry:

- 2 tablespoons peanut or vegetable oil
- 1½ pounds green beans, trimmed and rinsed
- 2 tablespoons water

For dietary purposes, please note that this recipe contains alcohol.

1. **Make Stir-Fry Sauce:** Combine the Stir-Fry Sauce ingredients in a small bowl. Set aside.

2. **Make Stir-Fry:** In a large skillet or wok, heat the oil and stir-fry the green beans until they are barely crisp (approximately 2 minutes).

3. Add water and continue stir-frying another 2 minutes until the beans are slightly tender and water has evaporated.

4. Add the sauce and continue stir-frying 5 to 6 minutes, until the beans are tender but not overcooked. Serve immediately.

Makes 6 Servings

Nutrients per Serving:
Calories 90 (Calories from Fat 40), Protein 3g, Fat 5g (Saturated Fat 1g), Carbohydrates 10g, Fiber 4g, Cholesterol 0mg, Sodium 310mg, Sugars 3g

Sweet Potato Bisque with Apple-Bacon Chutney and Spicy Texas Pecans

1 **tablespoon olive oil**

2 **slices bacon, diced**

½ **cup diced onion**

½ **cup diced carrots**

½ **cup diced celery**

4 **cloves garlic, peeled and minced**

½ **cup fresh orange juice**

2 **medium sweet potatoes, peeled and diced**

4 **new potatoes, peeled and diced**

6 **cups flavorful chicken or vegetable stock**

1 **tablespoon SPLENDA® Sugar Blend**

½ **teaspoon cayenne pepper**

Salt and freshly ground black pepper

Apple-Bacon Chutney, for garnish (recipe on page 56)

Spicy Texas Pecans, for garnish (recipe on page 57)

1. Heat oil in a large pan over medium-high heat; add bacon.

2. Cook about 2 minutes to render the fat.

3. Add onion, carrot, celery, and garlic. Sauté 5 to 7 minutes, stirring frequently. Add orange juice and reduce to thick syrup.

4. Add potatoes and stock; bring to a boil.

5. Reduce heat and simmer about 30 minutes or until potatoes are tender.

6. Add SPLENDA® Sugar Blend and cayenne.

7. Ladle mixture into a blender and purée thoroughly in batches; strain and season with salt and pepper. If the soup is too thick, thin with a little chicken or vegetable stock.

8. Serve warm and garnish with Apple-Bacon Chutney and Spicy Texas Pecans (see separate recipes).

Makes 8 Servings

Nutrients per Serving:
Calories 180 (Calories from Fat 45), Protein 5g, Fat 5g (Saturated Fat 1g), Carbohydrates 29g, Fiber 3g, Cholesterol 0mg, Sodium 860mg, Sugars 8g

PREP TIME: **10 Minutes**
COOK TIME: **25 Minutes**
TOTAL TIME: **35 Minutes**

Apple-Bacon Chutney

1½ **cups apple cider vinegar**

¾ **cup SPLENDA® Sugar Blend**

1 **cup smoked bacon, diced**

2 **green apples (pippin or Granny Smith) cored and diced**

2 **tablespoons lemon juice**

½ **cup onion, diced**

2 **tablespoons red bell pepper, diced**

2 **tablespoons green bell pepper, diced**

Salt

1. Combine vinegar and SPLENDA® Sugar Blend in a large saucepan. Cook over high heat for 8 to 10 minutes, whisking for the first 30 seconds to dissolve. Mixture should be quite thick.

2. Cook the diced bacon in a small skillet over medium-high heat for 3 to 5 minutes, until the fat renders. Drain the bacon.

3. Add bacon to the SPLENDA® Sugar Blend and vinegar mixture with remaining ingredients, except salt. Cook about 10 minutes more, until liquid has reduced and is quite thick.

4. Remove from heat, let cool completely. Season with salt.

Makes 16 Servings

Nutrients per Serving:
Calories 80 (Calories from Fat 15), Protein 1g, Fat 2g (Saturated Fat 1g), Carbohydrates 13g, Fiber 0g, Cholesterol 5mg, Sodium 85mg, Sugars 13g

Spicy Texas Pecans

2 tablespoons unsalted butter

3 cups pecan halves

¼ cup SPLENDA® Sugar Blend

1 teaspoon paprika

2 teaspoons pure chili powder

1 tablespoon ground cumin

¼ cup apple cider vinegar

Salt (optional)

1. Preheat oven to 325°F.
2. Melt butter in a large skillet over high heat.
3. Add pecans and sauté until lightly browned, about 3 minutes.
4. Add SPLENDA® Sugar Blend; cook until caramelized, about 3 to 5 minutes, stirring constantly.
5. Stir in paprika, chili powder, and cumin. Add vinegar and cook until liquid has evaporated; season with salt, if desired.
6. Spread pecans on a cookie sheet; bake in preheated oven until crisp, about 3 minutes.

Makes 16 Servings

Nutrients per Serving:
Calories 170 (Calories from Fat 150), Protein 2g, Fat 16g (Saturated Fat 2g), Carbohydrates 6g, Fiber 2g, Cholesterol 5mg, Sodium 30mg, Sugars 4g

Curried Turkey and Apple Salad

- 1 **tablespoon canola oil**
- 1 **tablespoon curry powder**
- ¼ **cup diced onion**
- 2 **tablespoons fresh lemon juice**
- 2 **tablespoons SPLENDA® No Calorie Sweetener, Granulated**
- ¼ **teaspoon salt (optional)**
- ¼ **cup low-fat mayonnaise**
- 2 **stalks celery, thinly sliced**
- 1 **medium apple, cut into chunks**
- 1 **pound roasted turkey breast, chopped into bite-size chunks**
  Salad greens
- ⅓ **cup chopped dried apricots**

1. Place oil, curry powder, and onion in a small saucepan. Heat on medium high heat. Simmer 1 to 2 minutes or until onions are tender. Add lemon juice, SPLENDA® Granulated Sweetener, and salt. Simmer over medium heat approximately 1 minute or until sauce begins to thicken. Remove from heat and cool.

2. Add mayonnaise to cooled sauce. Stir well. Place prepared salad ingredients in a large bowl. Toss with dressing until evenly coated.

3. Serve on salad greens. Garnish with a sprinkling of chopped apricots.

Makes 4 Servings

Nutrients per Serving:
Calories 270 (Calories from Fat 50), Protein 35g, Fat 6g (Saturated Fat 1g), Carbohydrates 20g, Fiber 3g, Cholesterol 95mg, Sodium 380mg, Sugars 14g

Tasty Teriyaki Chicken

1 **tablespoon cornstarch**

1 **tablespoon cold water**

½ **cup SPLENDA®
No Calorie Sweetener,
Granulated**

½ **cup soy sauce**

¼ **cup cider vinegar**

1 **clove garlic, minced**

½ **teaspoon ground
ginger**

¼ **teaspoon ground black
pepper**

12 **skinless, boneless
chicken breast halves**

1. In a small saucepan over low heat, combine cornstarch, cold water, SPLENDA® Granulated Sweetener, soy sauce, vinegar, garlic, ginger, and ground black pepper. Simmer, stirring frequently, until sauce thickens and bubbles.

2. Preheat oven to 425°F.

3. Place chicken breasts in a lightly greased 9×13-inch baking dish. Brush chicken with the sauce. Turn pieces over and brush again.

4. Bake in the preheated oven 30 minutes. Turn pieces over, and bake for another 30 minutes, until no longer pink and juices run clear. Brush with sauce every 10 minutes during cooking.

Makes 12 Servings

Nutrients per Serving:
Calories 140 (Calories from Fat 25), Protein 25g, Fat 3g (Saturated Fat 1g),
Carbohydrates 3g, Fiber 0g, Cholesterol 65mg, Sodium 670mg, Sugars 2g

Chili Vegetarian Style

1 **tablespoon extra-virgin olive oil**

1 **jalapeño pepper, seeded and finely chopped**

½ **cup chopped onion**

1⅓ **cups chopped red and yellow bell peppers**

6 **teaspoons chili powder**

1½ **teaspoons paprika**

¼ **teaspoon garlic powder**

¾ **teaspoon ground cayenne pepper**

½ **cup SPLENDA® No Calorie Sweetener, Granulated**

3 **tablespoons balsamic vinegar**

1 **(28-ounce) can crushed tomatoes with thick tomato purée**

1 **(19-ounce) can black beans, undrained**

2 **(19-ounce) cans dark red kidney beans, undrained**

1 **(19-ounce) can cannellini beans, undrained**

1 **(10-ounce) package frozen whole kernel corn**

1. In a large nonstick stockpot, heat olive oil. Sauté jalapeño pepper, onion, and red and yellow peppers over medium heat until onions are translucent (5 to 8 minutes).

2. Add the remaining ingredients and slowly bring to a boil. Cover pot and simmer on low heat for 20 minutes. Serve hot.

Makes 16 Servings

Nutrients per Serving:
Calories 160 (Calories from Fat 15), Protein 9g, Fat 2g (Saturated Fat 0g),
Carbohydrates 30g, Fiber 10g, Cholesterol 0mg, Sodium 500mg, Sugars 3g

Raspberry Cocktail Sauce with Chilled Shrimp

Cocktail Sauce:

- 1 cup no-sugar-added raspberry preserves
- ¼ cup prepared horseradish
- 3 tablespoons SPLENDA® No Calorie Sweetener, Granulated
- 2 tablespoons tomato paste
- 3 teaspoons sherry wine vinegar
- 2 tablespoons Worcestershire sauce
- 1 clove garlic, minced
- 1 jalapeño pepper, minced
- ½ teaspoon salt
- 1 pinch black pepper

- 2 pounds cooked, peeled and deveined shrimp

1. Place cocktail sauce ingredients in a food processor or a blender. Process or blend for 30 seconds or until smooth.
2. Chill cocktail sauce at least 2 hours before serving. Serve with shrimp. Cocktail sauce will keep, refrigerated, for 5 days.

Makes 32 Servings

Nutrients per Serving:
Calories 45 (Calories from Fat 0), Protein 6g, Fat 0g (Saturated Fat 0g), Carbohydrates 4g, Fiber 1g, Cholesterol 55mg, Sodium 125mg, Sugars 3g

Splenda.

Spring Greens with Citrus Vinaigrette

Dressing:

- 1 **teaspoon cornstarch**
- 3 **tablespoons SPLENDA®
  No Calorie Sweetener,
  Granulated**
- ¼ **cup water**
- 2 **teaspoons grated
  orange peel**
- 1 **tablespoon fresh
  orange juice**
- 1 **tablespoon fresh lime
  juice**
- ¼ **cup white wine vinegar**
- ½ **cup canola oil**
- 1 **teaspoon salt**
- ⅛ **teaspoon ground white
  pepper**

- 5 **ounces baby salad
  greens**

1. Mix cornstarch, SPLENDA® Granulated Sweetener, and water in a small saucepan. Heat over medium-high heat. Stir constantly until mixture thickens. Set aside to cool, approximately 10 minutes.
2. Place orange peel, orange juice, lime juice, and vinegar in blender; mix briefly on high.
3. Turn blender to low; drizzle oil into juice mixture. Add starch mixture to juice mixture; briefly blend on low.
4. Season with salt and pepper.
5. Toss dressing with greens. Refrigerate remaining dressing up to 5 days.

Makes 10 Servings

Chopped Salad with Buttermilk Poppy Seed Dressing

Dressing:

- 1 cup buttermilk
- 1 tablespoon cornstarch
- ¼ teaspoon SPLENDA® No Calorie Sweetener, Granulated
- 2 tablespoons Dijon-style mustard
- 2 tablespoons reduced-fat mayonnaise
- ¼ teaspoon salt
- 2 teaspoons poppy seeds

Salad:

- 8 cups chopped romaine lettuce
- 1 avocado, slightly ripe and slightly firm to the touch
- 1 cup coarsely chopped jicama

- 4 ounces sliced turkey breast
- ½ cup chopped red pepper
- 4 strips turkey bacon, cooked
- 2 tablespoons crumbled blue cheese
- ⅓ cup frozen yellow corn kernels, thawed

1. **Prepare Dressing:** Pour half of the buttermilk into a small saucepan. Add the cornstarch and stir well, using a wire whisk. Stir until the cornstarch is fully incorporated and there are no lumps. Cook over medium heat until thickened and bubbling (about 3 to 4 minutes). Remove from heat. Pour buttermilk mixture into a medium bowl. Add remaining buttermilk, SPLENDA® Granulated Sweetener, mustard, mayonnaise, and salt. Stir well. Add poppy seeds and stir well. Cover and refrigerate at least 1 hour or until ready to use.

2. **Prepare salad:** Place romaine in a large mixing bowl and set aside. Slice avocado in half. Remove pit. Peel avocado or scoop avocado out of the skin with a large spoon. Chop avocado into approximately ½-inch chunks. Place in the bowl with the romaine lettuce. Add jicama and toss. Refrigerate romaine salad blend until ready to use. Set aside.

Splenda

Nutrients per Serving:
Calories 180 (Calories from Fat 100), Protein 9g, Fat 11g (Saturated Fat 2g), Carbohydrates 14g, Fiber 5g, Cholesterol 20mg, Sodium 660mg, Sugars 4g

Cut the sliced turkey breast into small strips. Toss with about 2 tablespoons of the chilled dressing and refrigerate until ready to use.

. Chop the red pepper into thin, 1-inch-long strips. Set aside.

. Chop the cooked bacon into short crosswise strips. Set aside.

. **Assemble salad:** Toss $^2/_3$ cup dressing with the romaine salad blend. Place on a serving platter. Place turkey in the center of the salad. Sprinkle over the entire salad the strips of bacon, blue cheese, corn, and red pepper strips. Serve immediately. Serve any remaining dressing on the side.

Makes 6 Servings

Baked Salmon with Orange-Ginger Sauce

2½-inch piece fresh
   ginger root

1 cup fresh orange juice

¼ cup SPLENDA®
   No Calorie Sweetener,
   Granulated

2 tablespoons fat-free
   half and half

¼ teaspoon cornstarch

¼ teaspoon salt
   (optional)

2 tablespoons unsalted
   butter, softened

2 cups frozen stir-fry
   vegetable blend

2 (4-ounce) salmon fillets

1. Preheat oven to 450°F.

2. **Prepare sauce:** Peel ginger root and slice into 10 slices. Pour orange juice into a small saucepan. Add SPLENDA® Granulated Sweetener and ginger root. Bring to a rolling boil over medium high heat. Boil 10 to 12 minutes or until orange juice has reduced to approximately 2 tablespoons. Remove sauce from heat. Remove ginger slices using a fork and discard. Set sauce aside.

3. Mix together the half and half, cornstarch, and salt. Set aside. Whisk the softened butter, 1 tablespoon at a time, into the 2 tablespoons of orange juice. Stir until melted. Add half and half mixture. Stir well. Place saucepan back on heat. Heat over medium-high heat until boiling.

4. Remove sauce from heat and mix in a blender 15 to 20 seconds or until smooth and lighter in color. Set aside.

5. **Prepare salmon:** Place vegetables in an 8×8-inch square baking pan. Place salmon fillets on top of the vegetables. Bake in preheated oven 10 to 15 minutes or until cooked through, but still tender.

6. Place vegetables and salmon on serving plates. Pour sauce over salmon. Serve immediately. Serve with steamed rice, if desired.

Makes 2 Servings

Nutrients per Serving:
Calories 440 (Calories from Fat 180), Protein 30g, Fat 20g (Saturated Fat 8g), Carbohydrates 38g, Fiber 7g, Cholesterol 95mg, Sodium 440mg, Sugars 14g

Fluffy Carrot Soufflé

1 **pound baby carrots**

2 **cups water**

½ **teaspoon salt**

¼ **cup butter**

3 **tablespoons
all-purpose flour**

1 **teaspoon baking
powder**

¼ **cup SPLENDA®
No Calorie Sweetener,
Granulated**

3 **large eggs**

1 **teaspoon vanilla
extract**

1. Preheat oven to 350°F.

2. Combine carrots, water, and salt in a medium
saucepan; bring to a boil. Reduce heat and
cook, covered, 12 to 15 minutes or until
carrots are tender. Drain.

3. Process carrots and butter in a food processor
until smooth, stopping once to scrape down
sides.

4. Combine flour, baking powder, and SPLENDA®
Granulated Sweetener; add to carrot mixture
and process until blended. Add eggs, one at
a time, and process until blended. Add vanilla
and pulse 2 or 3 times.

5. Spoon mixture into a greased 1-quart baking
dish.

6. Bake in preheated oven 30 to 45 minutes or
until thoroughly heated.

7. Serve immediately.

Makes 5 Servings

Nutrients per Serving:
Calories 180 (Calories from Fat 120), Protein 5g, Fat 13g (Saturated Fat 7g),
Carbohydrates 13g, Fiber 2g, Cholesterol 150mg, Sodium 450mg, Sugars 6g

Breast of Chicken with Manchamantal Sauce (Red Mole)

1 ounce guajillo, seeded and deveined

1½ ounces anchos, seeded and deveined

7 cups chicken stock

1½ pounds chicken breast, skinless and boneless

1 pound plum tomatoes

½ cup onions

4 cloves garlic, roasted

¼ cup fried plantains

1 tablespoon raisins

1 slice bread or challah

1 stick Mexican cinnamon

2 black peppercorns

2 cloves, whole

1 allspice, whole

½ tablespoon salt

1 cup fresh pineapple

1 large apple, cored and coarsely chopped

2 tablespoons sunflower oil

1 cup SPLENDA® No Calorie Sweetener, Granulated

1. Boil water in a 3-quart saucepan to soak the chilies.

2. Blister the chilies on a dry Comal or cast-iron frying pan over medium heat. Place the chilies in a medium mixing bowl, pour the boiling water over and soak for 20 minutes.

3. Remove chilies from water and use a blender with a little of the chili water, as needed, to purée.

4. Press the blended mixture through a food mill or sieve to remove skins and set mixture aside.

5. Heat chicken stock in a heavy 4-quart stockpot.

6. Poach chicken in the stock over low heat for 35 to 45 minutes. Reserve the stock and set chicken aside on a plate.

7. Roast tomatoes in a pan over medium heat for 10 to 15 minutes. Remove tomatoes from pan to drain. Roast onions and garlic in same pan.

8. Blend tomatoes, fried plantains, raisins, onions, garlic, bread, cinnamon, peppercorns, cloves, allspice, salt and 2 cups of the reserved stock until puréed and smooth, place in bowl and set aside.

Nutrients per Serving:
Calories 310 (Calories from Fat 130), Protein 25g, Fat 14g (Saturated Fat 3g), Carbohydrates 22g, Fiber 3g, Cholesterol 55mg, Sodium 1830mg, Sugars 11g

). Purée pineapple and apple together. Set aside.

). Heat sunflower oil until smoking in a heavy 6-quart stockpot and pan-fry the chili mixture. Stirring constantly for 10 to 15 minutes, add the blended tomato mixture, and continue to cook and stir for about 10 minutes. Add SPLENDA® Granulated Sweetener and fry 15 minutes more (thin with stock as needed). Stir in the pineapple and apple purée. Continue cooking until the mole is thick enough to coat the back of a spoon.

1. Place chicken in a wide bowl and ladle the mole over it.

Polynesian Pork Chops

½ **cup vegetable oil**

6 **lean pork chops**

2 **large eggs**

1 **cup all-purpose flour**

1 **(29-ounce) can diced peaches with heavy syrup**

½ **cup SPLENDA® Brown Sugar Blend**

½ **cup water, or as needed**

1. Heat oil in a skillet over medium heat.

2. Clean and de-bone the pork chops. In bowl, whisk eggs and set aside. In another bowl, add flour and any additional spices, if desired. Dip pork chops in egg and then flour.

3. Place the coated pork chops into the frying pan.

4. Cook for 25 minutes, turning as needed.

5. Turn the heat to low and add the peaches and SPLENDA® Brown Sugar Blend to the skillet on top of pork chops. Add water if it looks too dry.

6. Simmer for 10 minutes and serve.

Makes 6 Servings

Nutrients per Serving:
Calories 590 (Calories from Fat 240), Protein 34g, Fat 27g (Saturated Fat 6g), Carbohydrates 48g, Fiber 2g, Cholesterol 145mg, Sodium 85mg, Sugars 30g

Classic
Cookies & Bars

Splenda

Sweetness
is the most
important
ingredient
for life.

Peanut Butter and Jelly Bites

Peanut Butter Balls:

- **1 stick SPLENDA®**
  No Calorie Sweetener
  Flavors for Coffee,
  Caramel

- **1 stick SPLENDA®**
  No Calorie Sweetener
  Flavors for Coffee,
  French Vanilla

- **1 tablespoon sugar-free**
  cocoa mix

- **1 tablespoon graham**
  cracker crumbs

- **2 tablespoons peanut**
  butter

- **1½ teaspoons fat-free**
  cream cheese

Garnish:

- **2 tablespoons graham**
  cracker crumbs

- **2 teaspoons sugar-free**
  or no-sugar-added
  jam

1. Mix all peanut butter ball ingredients together in a small bowl. Roll into 6 balls. Roll balls in graham cracker crumbs.

2. Press a small indentation in center with fingertip. Fill with jelly. Serve immediately.

Makes 2 Servings

Nutrients per Serving:
Calories 150 (Calories from Fat 80), Protein 6g, Fat 9g (Saturated Fat 2g), Carbohydrates 15g, Fiber 1g, Cholesterol 0mg, Sodium 170mg, Sugars 5g

Old Fashioned Peanut Butter Chocolate Chip Cookies

- **1½ cups all-purpose flour**
- **1 teaspoon baking soda**
- **1 cup butter or margarine, softened**
- **½ cup creamy or chunky peanut butter**
- **½ cup SPLENDA® Sugar Blend**
- **½ cup SPLENDA® Brown Sugar Blend, packed**
- **1 teaspoon vanilla extract**
- **1 large egg**
- **1⅓ cups NESTLE® TOLL HOUSE® Peanut Butter & Milk Chocolate Morsels**

1. Preheat oven to 375°F.
2. Combine flour and baking soda in small bowl. Set aside.
3. Beat butter, peanut butter, SPLENDA® Sugar Blend, SPLENDA® Brown Sugar Blend, and vanilla extract in large bowl until creamy. Beat in egg. Gradually beat in flour mixture. Stir in morsels.
4. Drop dough by rounded tablespoons onto ungreased baking sheets. Press down slightly with bottom of glass dipped in SPLENDA® Sugar Blend.
5. Bake in preheated oven 8 to 10 minutes or until edges are set but centers are still soft. Cool on baking sheets 4 minutes. Remove to wire racks to cool completely.

Makes 36 Servings

Nutrients per Serving:
Calories 120 (Calories from Fat 70), Protein 2g, Fat 7g (Saturated Fat 4g), Carbohydrates 11g, Fiber 0g, Cholesterol 20mg, Sodium 105mg, Sugars 7g

Chunky Peanut Butter Triangles

1½ **cups all-purpose flour**

½ **teaspoon baking soda**

¾ **cup creamy or chunky peanut butter**

½ **cup light butter, softened**

¼ **cup SPLENDA® Sugar Blend**

⅓ **cup SPLENDA® Brown Sugar Blend, packed**

1 **large egg**

1 **teaspoon vanilla extract**

1 **(11.5-ounce) package NESTLE® TOLL HOUSE® Semi-Sweet Chocolate Chunks**

1. Preheat oven to 350°F.

2. Combine flour and baking soda in small bowl. Set aside.

3. Combine peanut butter, butter, SPLENDA® Sugar Blend, and SPLENDA® Brown Sugar Blend in large bowl; beat at medium speed until creamy. Beat in egg and vanilla. Gradually beat in flour mixture. Stir in chocolate chunks. Press into ungreased 13×9-inch baking pan, distributing chocolate chunks evenly.

4. Bake in preheated oven 18 to 20 minutes or until center is set. Cool completely in pan on wire rack. Cut into bars; slice each bar in half diagonally.

Makes 42 Servings

Nutrients per Serving:
Calories 110 (Calories from Fat 50), Protein 2g, Fat 6g (Saturated Fat 3g), Carbohydrates 12g, Fiber 1g, Cholesterol 10mg, Sodium 50mg, Sugars 8g

Dulce de Leche Sandwich Cookie

Dulce de Leche:

- 1½ **cups unsweetened soy milk**
- ¼ **cup SPLENDA® Brown Sugar Blend**
- ½ **cup SPLENDA® No Calorie Sweetener, Granulated**
- 1 **tablespoon vanilla extract**
- ¼ **teaspoon baking powder**

Cookies:

- ¾ **cup all-purpose flour**
- 1 **teaspoon ground cinnamon**
- 1 **cup SPLENDA® No Calorie Sweetener, Granulated**
- ¼ **cup SPLENDA® Brown Sugar Blend**
- ¼ **cup chilled margarine**
- 2 **tablespoons unsweetened soy milk**

1. **Prepare Dulce de Leche:** Heat soy milk over medium heat until it comes to a simmer.

2. Whisk in all other ingredients. Continue to simmer for approximately 30 minutes or until desired caramel consistency is achieved. Remove from heat and set aside. Keep warm.

3. **Prepare Cookies:** Preheat oven to 375°F. Line cookie sheets with parchment paper.

4. Sift flour and cinnamon into a medium sized mixing bowl. Mix in SPLENDA® Granulated Sweetener and SPLENDA® Brown Sugar Blend.

5. Rub margarine into flour mixture until crumbly. Add soy milk and mix until mixture forms a dough. Roll dough out on a floured surface to ⅛ inch thick. Cut dough into 2-inch-wide circles using a round cookie cutter.

6. Place rounds on an ungreased cookie lined with parchment paper.

7. Bake for approximately 20 minutes or until lightly golden brown on the edges. Allow cookies to cool for 3 minutes.

8. Spread each cookie with 1 tablespoon of Dulce de Leche. Sandwich 2 cookies together. Serve warm.

Makes 5 Servings

Nutrients per Serving:
Calories 300 (Calories from Fat 100), Protein 4g, Fat 11g (Saturated Fat 2g), Carbohydrates 42g, Fiber 2g, Cholesterol 0mg, Sodium 140mg, Sugars 26g

Coconutty Bars

½ **cup butter**

½ **cup SPLENDA®
Brown Sugar Blend,
packed, divided**

1 **cup all-purpose flour**

2 **large eggs**

1 **teaspoon vanilla
extract**

2 **tablespoons
all-purpose flour**

½ **teaspoon baking
powder**

1½ **cups coconut**

1 **cup chopped pecans**

1. Preheat oven to 350°F.

2. Combine butter, ¼ cup SPLENDA® Brown Sugar Blend, and flour until a dough forms. Press into a 13×9-inch baking pan.

3. Bake in preheated oven 10 minutes.

4. Blend eggs, remaining ¼ cup SPLENDA® Brown Sugar Blend, vanilla, flour, and baking powder. Stir in the coconut and the pecans.

5. Spread the filling onto pre-baked crust.

6. Return to preheated oven for 20 minutes.

Makes 18 Servings

Nutrients per Serving:
Calories 210 (Calories from Fat 140), Protein 3g, Fat 16g (Saturated Fat 8g), Carbohydrates 14g, Fiber 2g, Cholesterol 35mg, Sodium 70mg, Sugars 6g

Merry Gingerbread Cookies

- 6 **cups all-purpose flour**
- 1 **teaspoon baking soda**
- ½ **teaspoon baking powder**
- 4 **teaspoons ground ginger**
- 4 **teaspoons ground cinnamon**
- 1½ **teaspoons ground cloves**
- 1 **cup unsalted butter, softened**
- 1 **cup SPLENDA® No Calorie Sweetener, Granulated**
- 1 **teaspoon salt**
- 2 **large eggs**
- 1 **cup molasses**
- 3 **tablespoons water**

1. Blend together flour, baking soda, baking powder, and spices in a large mixing bowl.
2. Cream butter, SPLENDA® Granulated Sweetener, and salt together in a large mixing bowl. Add eggs, one at a time, beating well after each addition. Add the molasses and water. Stir well. Add the flour mixture and stir until well blended. Refrigerate dough 1 to 2 hours before rolling out and cutting into shapes.
3. Preheat oven to 350°F. Roll cookie dough out slightly less than ¼ inch thick. Cut into desired shapes. Bake in preheated oven 8 to 10 minutes or until lightly browned on the bottom.

Makes 54 Servings

Nutrients per Serving:
Calories 100 (Calories from Fat 35), Protein 2g, Fat 4g (Saturated Fat 2g), Carbohydrates 15g, Fiber 1g, Cholesterol 15mg, Sodium 75mg, Sugars 4g

Chocolate Chip Pumpkin Bars

1⅓ **cups all-purpose flour**

¼ **cup SPLENDA®
Brown Sugar Blend**

½ **cup SPLENDA®
Sugar Blend, divided**

1 **cup old-fashioned oats**

½ **cup chopped walnuts
or pecans**

¾ **cup light margarine**

1 **(8-ounce) container
fat-free cream cheese**

3 **large eggs**

1 **(15-ounce) can
pumpkin**

1 **tablespoon pumpkin
pie spice**

1 **cup mini chocolate
chips**

1. Preheat oven to 350°F. Line a 13×9-inch pan with foil and spray with a nonstick cooking spray. Set aside.

2. Combine flour, SPLENDA® Brown Sugar Blend, half of the SPLENDA® Sugar Blend, oats, and walnuts. Cut in margarine with a fork until the mixture is crumbly.

3. Press all but 1 cup of the crust mixture into the bottom of the prepared pan.

4. Bake in preheated oven 15 minutes. Allow to cool.

5. Beat cream cheese, eggs, the remaining half of the SPLENDA® Sugar Blend, pumpkin, and the pumpkin pie spice until it is well blended.

6. Pour the cream cheese mixture over the pre-baked crust and sprinkle with the remaining 1 cup crust mixture and chocolate chips.

7. Return to preheated oven an additional 25 minutes or until set. Lift from pan to cool. Cut into 24 bars.

Makes 24 Servings

Nutrients per Serving:
Calories 150 (Calories from Fat 45), Protein 4g, Fat 5g (Saturated Fat 2g), Carbohydrates 21g, Fiber 2g, Cholesterol 25mg, Sodium 150mg, Sugars 12g

Coconut-Date-Nut Balls

¾ **cup flaked coconut**

½ **cup butter**

1 **(8-ounce) package dates, chopped**

¾ **cup chopped pecans**

½ **cup egg substitute**

¾ **cup SPLENDA® No Calorie Sweetener, Granulated**

3½ **cups crispy rice cereal**

1. Preheat oven to 350°F. Bake coconut, stirring occasionally, 5 to 6 minutes or until toasted. Set aside.

2. Melt butter in a large skillet over low heat. Add dates and pecans; cook over low heat, stirring constantly until dates are softened. Cool to touch (about 5 minutes).

3. Beat egg substitute and SPLENDA® Granulated Sweetener for 3 minutes at medium speed with an electric mixer; add to date mixture. Cook over low heat, stirring constantly, until mixture thickens (about 3 minutes). Stir in rice cereal. Cool to touch. Shape into 1-inch balls. Roll in toasted coconut.

Makes 36 Servings

Nutrients per Serving:
Calories 80 (Calories from Fat 45), Protein 1g, Fat 5g (Saturated Fat 2g), Carbohydrates 8g, Fiber 1g, Cholesterol 5mg, Sodium 55mg, Sugars 5g

Oat-Date Bars

8 ounces chopped dates

¾ cup NESTLE® CARNATION® Lowfat 2% Evaporated Milk

1 tablespoon SPLENDA® Sugar Blend

1 teaspoon vanilla extract

1 cup all-purpose flour

¾ cup quick-cooking oats

½ teaspoon baking soda

½ teaspoon salt

½ teaspoon ground cinnamon

½ cup butter or margarine, softened

¼ cup SPLENDA® Brown Sugar Blend, packed

1. Preheat oven to 400°F. Spray an 8-inch square baking pan with nonstick cooking spray.

2. Combine dates, evaporated milk, SPLENDA® Sugar Blend, and vanilla in medium saucepan. Cook on medium-low heat, stirring occasionally, 8 to 10 minutes or until thickened. Remove from heat.

3. Combine flour, oats, baking soda, salt, and cinnamon in a medium bowl; set aside.

4. Combine butter and SPLENDA® Brown Sugar Blend in large bowl; beat at medium speed until creamy. Beat in flour mixture. With floured fingers, press half of crust mixture onto bottom of prepared baking pan. Spread date filling over crust. Top with remaining crust mixture.

5. Bake in preheated oven 20 to 25 minutes or until golden. Cut into bars. Serve warm.

Makes 16 Servings

Nutrients per Serving:
Calories 160 (Calories from Fat 60), Protein 3g, Fat 6g (Saturated Fat 4g),
Carbohydrates 24g, Fiber 2g, Cholesterol 20mg, Sodium 190mg, Sugars 14g

PREP TIME: **20 Minutes**
COOK TIME: **25 Minutes**
TOTAL TIME: **1 Hour,**
45 Minutes

Mama Mia's Hazelnut Biscotti

½ **cup chopped hazelnuts**

½ **cup canola oil**

⅔ **cup SPLENDA®**
No Calorie Sweetener,
Granulated

3 **tablespoons white**
granulated sugar

2 **large eggs**

3 **tablespoons sugar-free**
hazelnut syrup

2 **cups all-purpose flour**

¾ **teaspoon baking**
powder

½ **teaspoon baking soda**

⅓ **cup nonfat dry milk**

2 **tablespoons mini**
chocolate chips,
melted (optional)

1. Preheat oven to 350°F. Spray a cookie sheet or jellyroll pan with nonstick spray. Set aside.

2. Spread hazelnuts in a shallow pan and toast in preheated oven for 7 to 10 minutes. Remove hazelnuts from the oven and cool.

3. Mix the oil, SPLENDA® Granulated Sweetener, and sugar together in a large mixing bowl. Add eggs, one at a time, mixing well after each addition. Add hazelnut syrup and mix well. Set aside.

4. Mix flour, baking powder, baking soda, and nonfat dry milk in a medium mixing bowl.

5. Pour the flour mixture into the oil and egg mixture and stir until blended. Add hazelnuts and mix until just blended. Refrigerate dough 1 hour or until stiff.

6. Divide dough in half. Roll each half into a log approximately 3½ inches wide by 12 inches long. Place the logs on the prepared sheet 2 inches apart.

7. Bake in preheated oven 20 to 25 minutes.

8. Remove from oven and cool for 5 minutes. Cut the loaves with a sharp knife into 48 slices, approximately ½ inch wide. Cool completely.

9. If desired, lay slices on their sides and drizzle with melted chocolate chips.

10. Store in airtight containers. Cookies will stay fresh up to 5 days.

Makes 48 Servings

Nutrients per Serving:
Calories 60 (Calories from Fat 30), Protein 1g, Fat 3g (Saturated Fat 0g),
Carbohydrates 6g, Fiber 0g, Cholesterol 10mg, Sodium 30mg, Sugars 2g

Banana Bars with Cream Cheese Frosting

Banana Bars:

- 1⅔ cups all-purpose flour
- 1 teaspoon baking powder
- 1 teaspoon baking soda
- ¼ teaspoon salt
- 1⅓ cups mashed bananas
- 1⅓ cups 1% low-fat milk
- 2 tablespoons unsweetened pineapple juice
- 2 large eggs
- ¾ cup SPLENDA® No Calorie Sweetener, Granulated
- 6 tablespoons butter, melted
- 2 teaspoons vanilla extract
- ½ teaspoon banana extract

Cream Cheese Frosting:

- 2 (8-ounce) packages fat-free cream cheese
- ½ cup light butter, softened
- ⅓ cup SPLENDA® No Calorie Sweetener, Granulated
- 2 teaspoons vanilla extract

1. Preheat oven to 350°F. Lightly coat a 13×9×2-inch baking pan with nonstick cooking spray.

2. Combine flour, baking powder, soda, and salt. Set aside.

3. Combine mashed bananas, milk, and pineapple juice. Set aside.

4. Beat eggs and SPLENDA® Granulated Sweetener at high speed with an electric mixer for 5 minutes. Add melted butter, vanilla, and banana extract; beat at medium speed until blended, about 1 minute. Add flour mixture alternately with banana mixture, beginning and ending with flour mixture. Beat at low speed, just until blended after each addition; do not overmix. Spoon mixture into prepared pan.

5. Bake in preheated oven 25 minutes or until cake tester inserted in center comes out clean. Cool in pan on a wire rack.

6. Prepare Frosting: Beat cream cheese and butter at medium speed with an electric mixer until creamy. Gradually add SPLENDA® Granulated Sweetener, beating at medium speed until blended. Stir in vanilla. Spread over cooled bars. Chill 30 minutes before cutting into bars.

Makes 24 Servings

Nutrients per Serving:
Calories 120 (Calories from Fat 50), Protein 5g, Fat 6g (Saturated Fat 3g), Carbohydrates 13g, Fiber 1g, Cholesterol 35mg, Sodium 270mg, Sugars 5g

Deep Chocolate Shortbread

1 cup unsalted butter

**½ cup SPLENDA®
  No Calorie Sweetener,
  Granulated**

¼ cup sugar

**½ teaspoon vanilla
  extract**

¼ teaspoon salt

**6 tablespoons Dutch
  process cocoa powder**

**1¾ cups all-purpose flour
  plus 2 tablespoons
  all-purpose flour**

1. Preheat oven to 375°F. Line a cookie sheet or jellyroll pan with parchment paper. Set aside.

2. Place butter, SPLENDA® Granulated Sweetener, sugar, vanilla, and salt in a medium mixing bowl. Mix, using the paddle attachment of an electric mixer until the mixture is light and creamy (approximately 1 to 1½ minutes). Add cocoa powder and flour. Mix until just blended.

3. Remove dough from bowl and form into a ball. Place the ball of dough on the parchment-lined pan. Roll the dough into a rectangle approximately 6½ inches wide by 11 inches long and ¼ inch thick. Pierce the surface of the dough all over with a fork. This allows air to escape during baking preventing air pockets from forming.

4. Bake in preheated oven 20 to 25 minutes, rotating the pan after 10 minutes of baking. Remove shortbread from oven after 20 to 25 minutes and immediately cut into 24 fingers or rectangles while still warm. If allowed to cool, shortbread will not slice well.

Makes 24 Servings

Nutrients per Serving:
Calories 120 (Calories from Fat 70), Protein 1g, Fat 8g (Saturated Fat 5g), Carbohydrates 11g, Fiber 1g, Cholesterol 20mg, Sodium 25mg, Sugars 3g

Sand Tarts

- 1 **cup butter, softened**
- ¼ **cup SPLENDA®**
  No Calorie Sweetener,
  Granulated
- 2 **cups all-purpose flour**
- 2 **teaspoons vanilla**
  extract
- 1 **cup chopped pecans**
- 2 **tablespoons SPLENDA®**
  No Calorie Sweetener,
  Granulated
- 2 **teaspoons cornstarch**

1. Preheat oven to 350°F.
2. Beat butter and ¼ cup SPLENDA® Granulated Sweetener at medium speed with an electric mixer about 2 minutes or until creamy. Gradually add flour, beating at low speed until blended. Stir in vanilla and pecans. Shape into 1-inch balls.
3. Bake in preheated oven 20 minutes; remove from oven and place on wire racks to cool.
4. Process 2 tablespoons SPLENDA® Granulated Sweetener and cornstarch in a blender or food processor; roll cookies in powdered SPLENDA® Granulated Sweetener mixture.

Makes 42 Servings

Nutrients per Serving:
Calories 80 (Calories from Fat 60), Protein 1g, Fat 6g (Saturated Fat 3g), Carbohydrates 5g, Fiber 0g, Cholesterol 10mg, Sodium 45mg, Sugars 0g

After-School Butterscotch Brownies

2¼ **cups all-purpose flour**

1 **teaspoon baking powder**

½ **teaspoon salt**

1 **cup butter or margarine, softened**

¾ **cup SPLENDA® Brown Sugar Blend, packed**

1 **tablespoon vanilla extract**

2 **large eggs**

1 **(11-ounce) package NESTLE® TOLL HOUSE® Butterscotch Flavored Morsels, divided**

½ **cup chopped pecans**

1. Preheat oven to 350°F.

2. Combine flour, baking powder, and salt in medium bowl. Set aside.

3. Combine butter, SPLENDA® Brown Sugar Blend, and vanilla in a large mixer bowl; beat at medium speed until creamy. Beat in eggs. Gradually beat in flour mixture. Stir in 1 cup morsels and pecans. Spread into an ungreased 13×9-inch baking pan. Sprinkle with remaining ⅔ cup morsels.

4. Bake in preheated oven 30 to 40 minutes or until wooden pick inserted in center comes out clean. Cool in pan on wire rack. Cut into bars.

Makes 48 Servings

Nutrients per Serving:
Calories 120 (Calories from Fat 60), Protein 1g, Fat 7g (Saturated Fat 4g), Carbohydrates 12g, Fiber 0g, Cholesterol 20mg, Sodium 75mg, Sugars 7g

Peanut Butter Chocolate Cheesecake Cups

Crust:

- **36 reduced-fat chocolate wafers**
- **¼ cup SPLENDA® No Calorie Sweetener, Granulated**
- **5 tablespoons light butter, melted**

Peanut Butter Center:

- **½ cup SPLENDA® No Calorie Sweetener, Granulated**
- **3 tablespoons reduced-fat peanut butter**
- **3 tablespoons reduced-fat cream cheese**

Chocolate Filling:

- **4 ounces unsweetened chocolate**
- **8 ounces reduced-fat cream cheese**
- **1¾ cups SPLENDA® No Calorie Sweetener, Granulated**

- **½ cup skim milk**
- **½ cup egg substitute**
- **1 teaspoon vanilla**
- **2 ounces sugar-free chocolate, melted (optional)**

1. Preheat oven to 350°F.
2. Prepare Crust: Crush cookies into fine crumbs. Blend all crust ingredients together in a small bowl. Stir until well blended. Set aside.
3. Prepare Peanut Butter Center: Place center ingredients in a small bowl. Mix until well blended. Set aside.
4. Make Chocolate Filling: Melt chocolate in small saucepan over low heat. Set aside. Place cream cheese and SPLENDA® Granulated Sweetener in a small mixing bowl. Beat until soft. Slowly add skim milk. Mix, using a wire whisk, until smooth. Add melted chocolate. Stir well. Add egg substitute and vanilla. Mix until well blended. Set aside.
5. Assemble Cups: Place 24 mini-size foil baking cups on a sheet pan. Evenly divide crust between the 24 baking cups. Firmly press crusts into the bottom of the cups. Place approximately ½ teaspoon of the peanut butter center in the center of each crust-lined

Nutrients per Serving:
Calories 120 (Calories from Fat 70), Protein 3g, Fat 8g (Saturated Fat 4g),
Carbohydrates 11g, Fiber 1g, Cholesterol 10mg, Sodium 95mg, Sugars 5g

baking cup. Spoon chocolate filling into each baking cup. Firmly tap sheet pan on countertop to remove any air bubbles.

. Bake in a preheated oven 10 to 15 minutes, or until slightly firm to the touch. Chill for approximately 2 hours before serving. Drizzle optional melted chocolate over the top for a garnish.

Makes 24 Servings

Chocolate Chip Meringue Crisps

½ **cup chopped walnuts**

2 **egg whites**

½ **teaspoon vanilla
extract**

½ **cup SPLENDA®
Sugar Blend**

½ **cup semi-sweet
chocolate morsels**

1. Preheat oven to 200°F.

2. Bake walnuts in a shallow pan, stirring
occasionally, 5 minutes or until toasted.
Set aside.

3. Beat egg whites and vanilla at high speed
with an electric mixer until foamy.

4. Add SPLENDA® Sugar Blend, 1 tablespoon at
a time, beating until stiff peaks form; stir in
walnuts and chocolate morsels.

5. Spoon rounded teaspoons of mixture onto
baking sheets lined with parchment paper.

6. Bake in preheated oven 2 hours. Cool slightly
on cookie sheet. Remove to wire racks to cool
completely. Store in an airtight tin.

Makes 36 Servings

Nutrients per Serving:
Calories 35 (Calories from Fat 15), Protein 1g, Fat 2g (Saturated Fat 1g),
Carbohydrates 4g, Fiber 0g, Cholesterol 0mg, Sodium 0mg, Sugars 4g

Ginger Snaps

⅔ **cup SPLENDA® No Calorie Sweetener, Granulated**

¾ **cup sugar**

⅔ **cup unsalted butter**

⅓ **cup molasses***

2 **tablespoons canola oil**

¼ **cup egg substitute**

3¼ **cups all-purpose flour**

2 **teaspoons baking soda**

8 **teaspoons ground ginger**

½ **teaspoon ground cloves**

2 **teaspoons ground cinnamon**

Use Dark Molasses for a more robust molasses flavor.

1. Mix SPLENDA® Granulated Sweetener, sugar, butter, molasses, and oil together in a medium mixing bowl. Mix on medium speed until creamy. Scrape sides of the bowl. Add egg substitute and mix well. Add remaining ingredients and mix until blended.

2. Divide dough in half. Roll into logs approximately 1½ inches wide by 14 inches long. Cover with plastic wrap and refrigerate 3 hours or freeze 1½ hours or until firm.

3. Preheat oven to 350°F. Lightly oil cookie sheets.

4. Slice cookies approximately ¼ inch thick. Place on prepared sheets.**

5. Bake in preheated oven 10 to 12 minutes or until bottoms are lightly browned.

Cookie dough can also be rolled out and cut into circles or shapes.

Makes 36 Servings

Nutrients per Serving:
Calories 110 (Calories from Fat 40), Protein 1g, Fat 4g (Saturated Fat 2g), Carbohydrates 16g, Fiber 0g, Cholesterol 10mg, Sodium 75mg, Sugars 7g

Chocolate Toffee Bars

Crust:

- ¼ **cup unsalted butter, softened**
- ½ **cup SPLENDA® Brown Sugar Blend, firmly packed**
- 1 **egg yolk**
- 1 **cup all-purpose flour**
- ¼ **teaspoon salt**

Toffee:

- ¼ **cup unsalted butter, softened**
- 1 **cup SPLENDA® Brown Sugar Blend, firmly packed**
- ½ **cup light corn syrup**
- ½ **cup evaporated milk**
- 1½ **teaspoons vanilla extract**

Topping:

- 3 **(1-ounce) squares unsweetened chocolate, chopped**
- 2 **tablespoons SPLENDA® Brown Sugar Blend**
- 1 **cup chopped pecans, toasted**

1. Preheat oven to 350°F. Lightly spray a 13×9×2-inch baking pan with nonstick cooking spray.

2. Beat ¼ cup butter and ½ cup SPLENDA® Brown Sugar Blend at medium speed with an electric mixer until blended. Add egg yolk and beat until blended. Add flour and salt; beat on low speed until blended. Press mixture into bottom of prepared pan.

3. Bake crust in preheated oven 12 to 14 minutes or until golden. Cool in pan on a wire rack.

4. Prepare Toffee: Combine ¼ cup butter, 1 cup SPLENDA® Brown Sugar Blend, corn syrup, evaporated milk, and vanilla in medium saucepan. Cook over low heat, stirring constantly, until SPLENDA® Brown Sugar Blend dissolves. Bring mixture to a boil over medium heat and cook until candy thermometer reaches or 265°F. (about 10 minutes). Pour mixture over crust and spread evenly. Bake 10 additional minutes. Cool 5 minutes on a wire rack.

5. Prepare Topping: Combine chocolate squares and 2 tablespoons SPLENDA® Brown Sugar Blend in top of a double boiler; bring water to a boil. Cook until chocolate melts and mixture is blended. Drizzle or spread over toffee. Sprinkle with chopped pecans. Cool completely on wire rack. When chocolate is firm, cut into bars or diamond shapes. Store in an airtight container.

Makes 30 Servings

Nutrients per Serving:
Calories 160 (Calories from Fat 70), Protein 2g, Fat 8g (Saturated Fat 3g), Carbohydrates 20g, Fiber 1g, Cholesterol 15mg, Sodium 30mg, Sugars 14g

PREP TIME: **5 Minutes**
COOK TIME: **13 Minutes**
TOTAL TIME: **20 Minutes**

Chocolate Chip Cookie

2 **cups all-purpose flour**

1 **teaspoon baking powder**

1 **teaspoon baking soda**

¼ **teaspoon salt**

1 **cup melted butter**

1 **cup SPLENDA® Brown Sugar Blend**

2 **large eggs**

1 **tablespoon vanilla**

2 **cups semi-sweet chocolate chips**

1. Preheat oven to 375°F. Line cookie sheets with parchment paper.

2. Combine flour, baking powder, baking soda, and salt in small bowl. Set aside.

3. Mix butter and SPLENDA® Brown Sugar Blend in a large bowl. Stir in eggs, one at a time. Add vanilla and mix. Stir in flour mixture. Fold in chocolate chips.

4. Drop dough by rounded tablespoons onto cookie sheets. Bake in preheated oven 11 to 13 minutes. Allow cookies to cool 2 minutes before moving to wire racks to cool completely.

Makes 30 Servings

Nutrients per Serving:
Calories 210 (Calories from Fat 100), Protein 2g, Fat 11g (Saturated Fat 7g), Carbohydrates 24g, Fiber 0g, Cholesterol 30mg, Sodium 140mg, Sugars 16g

Desserts for Every Day & Special Days

Splenda

Find your
inner
sweetness.

Fresh Strawberry Pie

⅓ **cup water**

1 **cup SPLENDA®**
   No Calorie Sweetener,
   Granulated

1 **(1-ounce) package**
   unflavored gelatin

⅓ **cup water**

6 **cups strawberries,**
   cleaned and cut in
   half

1 **(9-inch) prepared**
   reduced-fat graham
   cracker crust

1. Pour ⅓ cup water in a small mixing bowl. Add SPLENDA® Granulated Sweetener. Stir well. Sprinkle gelatin over the top. Let stand 1 minute.

2. Pour ⅓ cup water in a small pan. Boil. Pour boiling water over gelatin mixture. Stir until dissolved.

3. Refrigerate approximately 20 minutes or until the mixture begins to thicken. Stir frequently.

4. Toss with prepared berries and spoon into pie crust. Chill until set.

Makes 8 Servings

Nutrients per Serving:
Calories 140 (Calories from Fat 35), Protein 5g, Fat 4g (Saturated Fat 1g), Carbohydrates 22g, Fiber 3g, Cholesterol 0mg, Sodium 95mg, Sugars 6g

Individual Chocolate Crusted Cheesecakes

¾ cup chocolate wafer crumbs

1 (8-ounce) package fat-free cream cheese, softened

1 (8-ounce) package reduced-fat cream cheese, softened

½ cup SPLENDA® No Calorie Sweetener, Granulated

3 large eggs, separated

1 teaspoon vanilla extract

Optional Garnish: fresh raspberries

Topping:

½ cup fat-free sour cream

1 tablespoon SPLENDA® No Calorie Sweetener, Granulated

½ teaspoon vanilla extract

1. Preheat the oven to 350°F. Lightly spray 3 (12-cup) miniature muffin tins with nonstick cooking spray. Sprinkle each muffin cup with 1 teaspoon chocolate wafer crumbs. Turn pans upside down and discard excess. Set aside.

2. Beat cream cheese at high speed with an electric mixer until creamy; gradually add ½ cup SPLENDA® Granulated Sweetener, and beat at medium speed with an electric mixer about 2 minutes or until light and fluffy. Add egg yolks and vanilla; beat at low speed just until blended.

3. Beat egg whites until stiff peaks form. Gently fold into cream cheese mixture; spoon into prepared pans.

4. Bake in preheated oven 15 minutes.

5. Prepare Topping: Combine Topping ingredients; spoon about ½ teaspoon topping on each cheesecake. Bake in preheated oven 5 additional minutes. Remove to wire racks to cool. Chill thoroughly before removing from pan. Garnish, if desired.

Makes 36 Servings

Nutrients per Serving:
Calories 45 (Calories from Fat 20), Protein 3g, Fat 2g (Saturated Fat 1g), Carbohydrates 4g, Fiber 0g, Cholesterol 20mg, Sodium 75mg, Sugars 1g

Apple and Pear Crisp

Topping:

- ½ **cup all-purpose flour**
- 2 **tablespoons dark brown sugar**
- ¼ **cup SPLENDA® No Calorie Sweetener, Granulated**
- ¼ **teaspoon ground cinnamon**
- 1 **pinch ground nutmeg**
- 4 **tablespoons cold, unsalted butter, cut into pieces**

Filling:

- 4 **large Macintosh or other tart apples**
- 3 **Bartlett or Anjou pears**
- 2 **tablespoons SPLENDA® No Calorie Sweetener, Granulated**
- 3 **tablespoons apple juice concentrate**

1. Preheat the oven to 400°F. Lightly butter a deep 2- to 2½-quart baking dish. Set aside.

2. **Prepare Topping:** Pour flour, brown sugar, SPLENDA® Granulated Sweetener, cinnamon, and nutmeg into a medium mixing bowl. Stir well. Add butter and mix with an electric mixer, using the paddle attachment, until the topping is crumbly or sandy in texture. Set aside.

3. **Prepare Filling:** Peel, core, and thickly slice the apples and pears. Place them in the buttered baking dish. The fruit should be at least 2½ inches deep in the pan. Add more fruit, if necessary. Add SPLENDA® Granulated Sweetener and apple juice concentrate. Toss until coated. Cover with the topping.

4. Bake in preheated oven 40 to 50 minutes or until fruit is tender and the topping has browned.

Makes 8 Servings

Nutrients per Serving:
Calories 200 (Calories from Fat 60), Protein 1g, Fat 7g (Saturated Fat 4g),
Carbohydrates 38g, Fiber 5g, Cholesterol 15mg, Sodium 0mg, Sugars 25g

Tangy Coconut Tartlets

1½ **cups sweetened flaked coconut**

¼ **cup SPLENDA® No Calorie Sweetener, Granulated**

¾ **cup all-purpose flour**

2 **teaspoons vanilla extract**

2 **egg whites**

1 **(3.4-ounce) package instant lemon pudding mix**

2 **cups nonfat milk**

1 **(8-ounce) tub fat-free frozen whipped topping, thawed**

1 **tablespoon unsweetened flaked coconut, toasted**

1. Preheat oven to 400°F. Lightly grease 24 mini-muffin cups.

2. In a mixing bowl, combine 1½ cups coconut, SPLENDA® Granulated Sweetener, flour, vanilla, and egg whites; stir well. Divide mixture evenly among the prepared mini-muffin cups, pressing mixture into bottom and up sides of muffin cups.

3. Bake in the preheated oven until the edges are browned. Cool 2 minutes in the muffin tins on a wire rack. Remove from tins and cool completely on a wire rack.

4. Prepare lemon pudding mix according to package instructions using the milk. Spoon lemon mixture into each macaroon tartlet shell. Top with 2 teaspoons of whipped topping sprinkled with a pinch of toasted coconut.

Makes 24 Servings

Nutrients per Serving:
Calories 80 (Calories from Fat 15), Protein 2g, Fat 2g (Saturated Fat 1g), Carbohydrates 13g, Fiber 0g, Cholesterol 0mg, Sodium 85mg, Sugars 7g

Chocolate Velvet Mousse

3 ounces unsweetened chocolate

1 cup 1% low-fat milk

¼ cup egg substitute

½ cup SPLENDA® No Calorie Sweetener, Granulated

1 teaspoon cornstarch

2 tablespoons orange-flavored liqueur or brandy*

½ cup heavy cream

3 cups sliced strawberries

*For dietary purposes, please note that this recipe contains alcohol. Alcohol can be replaced with 1 teaspoon orange extract.

1. Place chocolate and milk in a medium saucepan. Heat over medium heat until chocolate melts. Set aside.

2. Stir together egg substitute, SPLENDA® Granulated Sweetener, cornstarch, and orange-flavored liqueur or brandy in a small mixing bowl. Add to chocolate mixture. Stir constantly. Cook over medium heat while stirring constantly until mixture begins to thicken (approximately 3 to 4 minutes). Remove from heat and pour into the bowl of a blender or food processor. Blend or process briefly (10 to 20 seconds) to make a more creamy texture. Pour into medium bowl and cover.

3. Refrigerate chocolate mixture approximately 2 to 3 hours or until cool. Whip cream until stiff and fold into chocolate. Refrigerate overnight to set. Will keep refrigerated 3 days.

4. To serve, layer strawberries and mousse in 6 all-purpose wine glasses.

Makes 6 Servings

Nutrients per Serving:
Calories 210 (Calories from Fat 150), Protein 5g, Fat 17g (Saturated Fat 10g), Carbohydrates 14g, Fiber 4g, Cholesterol 30mg, Sodium 50mg, Sugars 5g

Berry-Cherry Pie

1 (15-ounce) package
refrigerated pie crusts

1 (14.5-ounce) can pitted
tart red cherries,
undrained

1 (12-ounce) package
frozen raspberries,
thawed

1 cup fresh blueberries
or frozen blueberries,
thawed

1 cup SPLENDA® No
Calorie Sweetener,
Granulated

¼ cup cornstarch

2 tablespoons butter

Optional topping:

Frozen low-fat vanilla
yogurt

1. Preheat oven to 375°F.
2. Unfold 1 pie crust; press out fold lines. Fit
   pie crust into a 9-inch pie plate according to
   package directions.
3. Drain cherries, raspberries, and blueberries
   (if frozen), reserving 1 cup of the juices.
   Set berries and juice aside.
4. Combine SPLENDA® Granulated Sweetener
   and cornstarch in a medium saucepan;
   gradually stir in reserved juice. Cook over
   medium heat, stirring constantly, until
   mixture begins to boil. Boil 1 minute, stirring
   constantly. Stir in butter and reserved fruit.
   Cool slightly and spoon mixture into pie shell.
5. Unroll remaining pie crust; roll to ⅛-inch
   thickness. Place over filling. Fold edges under
   and crimp. Cut slits in top to allow steam to
   escape.
6. Bake in preheated oven 40 to 45 minutes or
   until crust is golden. Cover edges with foil to
   prevent excessive browning, if necessary. Cool
   on a wire rack. Serve with a scoop of frozen
   yogurt, if desired.

Makes 8 Servings

Nutrients per Serving:
Calories 330 (Calories from Fat 170), Protein 4g, Fat 19g (Saturated Fat 6g),
Carbohydrates 37g, Fiber 4g, Cholesterol 10mg, Sodium 290mg, Sugars 7g

Strawberry Panna Cottas

1½ **teaspoons unflavored gelatin**

1½ **cups whole milk**

1½ **pints strawberries, halved**

2 **tablespoons SPLENDA® No Calorie Sweetener, Granulated**

1 **teaspoon vanilla extract**

1 **pint strawberries, sliced**

1. Sprinkle gelatin over milk in a small saucepan; let stand 1 minute. Cook over low heat, stirring until gelatin dissolves (do not boil). Set aside to cool.

2. Process strawberries in a food processor until puréed, stopping to scrape down sides. Press strawberries through a fine wire-mesh strainer into a bowl, discarding solids. Stir cooled milk mixture into strawberry purée. Add SPLENDA® Granulated Sweetener and vanilla, stirring until SPLENDA® Granulated Sweetener dissolves.

3. Coat 4 (6-ounce) ramekins with nonstick cooking spray. Divide strawberry mixture evenly among ramekins. Cover each ramekin with plastic wrap; refrigerate 4 hours or overnight until panna cottas are set.

4. Run a knife around the edge of each panna cotta and unmold onto serving plates. Serve with sliced strawberries.

Makes 4 Servings

Nutrients per Serving:
Calories 130 (Calories from Fat 35), Protein 5g, Fat 4g (Saturated Fat 2g),
Carbohydrates 21g, Fiber 5g, Cholesterol 15mg, Sodium 50mg, Sugars 5g

Nostalgic Apple Pie

**1 (15-ounce) package
refrigerated pie crusts**

**7 cups baking apples,
thin-sliced, cored,
peeled**

**1 cup SPLENDA®
No Calorie Sweetener,
Granulated**

3 tablespoons cornstarch

**¾ teaspoon ground
cinnamon**

**¼ teaspoon ground
nutmeg**

⅛ teaspoon salt

1. Preheat oven to 425°F.

2. Unfold 1 pie crust; press out fold lines. Fit pie crust into a 9-inch pie plate according to package directions.

3. Place sliced apples into a large mixing bowl and set aside. Combine SPLENDA® Granulated Sweetener, cornstarch, cinnamon, nutmeg, and salt in a small bowl. Sprinkle mixture over apples and toss. Spoon apple mixture into pie crust. Place the second crust over the filling. Seal edges, trim, and flute. Make small openings in the top crust.

4. Bake in preheated oven 40 to 50 minutes or until the top crust is golden. Serve warm or chilled.

Makes 8 Servings

Nutrients per Serving:
Calories 300 (Calories from Fat 140), Protein 3g, Fat 15g (Saturated Fat 4g), Carbohydrates 40g, Fiber 5g, Cholesterol 0mg, Sodium 270mg, Sugars 14g

Banana Cream Angel Bites

Angel Bites:

5 egg whites

⅓ cup SPLENDA® No Calorie Sweetener, Granulated

1½ teaspoons vanilla extract

1 pinch salt

Banana Cream Filling:

½ cup egg substitute

1 cup nonfat milk

1 teaspoon vanilla extract

2 tablespoons light butter

1 tablespoon cornstarch

¼ cup SPLENDA® No Calorie Sweetener, Granulated

1 teaspoon banana flavor

2 bananas, sliced

2 ounces semisweet chocolate, shaved

1. Preheat oven to 350°F. Lightly oil a 13×11-inch baking sheet. Set aside.

2. **Prepare Angel Bites:** Place egg whites in a medium mixing bowl. Whip on high speed using an electric mixer or wire whisk until frothy.*

3. Add SPLENDA® Granulated Sweetener, vanilla, and salt. Mix on high speed until medium-stiff peaks form (approximately 20 to 30 seconds with an electric mixer).

4. Spoon rounded tablespoons of egg whites onto prepared baking sheet. Bake in preheated oven 10 to 15 minutes or until firm and golden brown. Remove from pan. Cool.

5. **Prepare Filling:** Place egg substitute, milk, vanilla, and light butter in a small saucepan. Blend cornstarch and SPLENDA® Granulated Sweetener together; add to ingredients in the saucepan. Stir well. Cook over medium heat, stirring constantly, until the mixture begins to thicken and bubble (approximately 3 to 4 minutes).

6. Remove filling from heat and add banana flavor. Stir until well mixed. For an extra creamy filling, pour into the bowl of a food processor or blender. Cover and process until very creamy (approximately 10 seconds). Pour filling into a bowl and refrigerate at least 20 minutes or until ready to serve.

Nutrients per Serving:
Calories 200 (Calories from Fat 60), Protein 10g, Fat 7g (Saturated Fat 4g), Carbohydrates 25g, Fiber 2g, Cholesterol 10mg, Sodium 230mg, Sugars 19g

Assemble Angel Bites: Just before serving, sandwich Angel Bites with filling. Place three Angel Bites on a plate with the bottoms facing up. Top each with sliced banana and a spoonful of filling. Stack another Angel Bite on top. Repeat for each serving.

Garnish with a dollop of whipped cream and chocolate shavings.**

---

*If egg whites start to separate, whisk them back together using a wire whisk.

****To Make Chocolate Shavings:** Scrape the edge of a chocolate bar with a vegetable peeler or melt chocolate and spread very thinly onto a cookie sheet. Cool at room temperature until firm. Scrape off cookie sheet with a spatula.

Makes 5 Servings

Cranberry-Almond Tarts

½ **(15-ounce) package refrigerated pie crusts**

¾ **cup SPLENDA® No Calorie Sweetener, Granulated**

⅓ **cup water**

1 **(12-ounce) bag fresh or frozen cranberries, thawed**

¼ **cup chopped almonds, toasted**

½ **teaspoon almond extract**

Non-dairy whipped topping (optional)

Toasted almond slices (optional)

1. Preheat oven to 375°F.

2. Unroll pie crusts and roll to ⅛-inch thickness on a lightly floured surface; using a 2-inch square cookie cutter, cut out 24 squares, re-rolling, if necessary. Place squares in ungreased mini-muffin pans. Place in freezer.

3. Combine SPLENDA® Granulated Sweetener and water in a saucepan, stirring until blended. Stir in cranberries. Bring mixture to a boil over medium-high heat. Cook, stirring constantly 2 minutes or until berries pop. Pour through a wire-mesh sieve, set over a bowl. Return liquid to saucepan; reserving berries. Bring liquid to a boil; reduce heat and simmer 5 minutes or until liquid is reduced to about 3 tablespoons. Pour sauce over cranberries, tossing to coat. Stir in almonds and almond extract. Spoon mixture into pastry shells.

4. Bake in preheated oven 15 to 20 minutes or until pastry is golden and filling is set. Carefully remove tarts from muffin tins; cool on a wire rack.

Makes 24 Servings

Nutrients per Serving:
Calories 100 (Calories from Fat 60), Protein 1g, Fat 6g (Saturated Fat 3g), Carbohydrates 9g, Fiber 1g, Cholesterol 0mg, Sodium 55mg, Sugars 3g

PREP TIME: **20 Minutes**
COOK TIME: **1 Hour,**
5 Minutes
TOTAL TIME: **7 Hours,**
25 Minutes

Dulce de Leche Cheesecake

Crust:

- **1 cup graham cracker crumbs***
- **3 tablespoons butter, melted**

Filling:

- **3 (8-ounce) packages reduced-fat cream cheese**
- **1 cup SPLENDA® No Calorie Sweetener, Granulated**
- **2 tablespoons all-purpose flour**
- **2 teaspoons vanilla extract**
- **3 large eggs**
- **⅓ cup 2% reduced-fat milk**
- **½ cup dulce de leche**

Graham cracker crumbs can be replaced with crushed vanilla wafers.

1. Preheat oven to 400°F.
2. **Prepare Crust:** Mix crust ingredients together and press into a 9-inch springform pan. Place pan on a baking sheet and bake in preheated oven 10 minutes. Remove from oven and cool to room temperature.
3. Reduce oven temperature to 325°F.
4. **Prepare Filling:** Beat cream cheese, SPLENDA® Granulated Sweetener, and flour together until well mixed and smooth. Add vanilla and mix until smooth. Add eggs, one at a time, beating well after each addition. Mix until smooth. Add milk and mix until well blended.
5. Measure ½ cup of the cheesecake batter and pour into a small bowl. Add dulce de leche and stir until well combined.
6. Pour plain batter over crust. Top with dulce de leche batter by placing rounded spoonfuls over the cheesecake batter and gently swirl into plain batter with the tip of knife or spatula.
7. Bake in preheated oven 45 to 55 minutes or until center is almost set. Remove from oven and gently run metal spatula around rim of pan to loosen cheesecake (this helps prevent cracking). Let cool 20 to 25 minutes before covering and placing in the refrigerator. Refrigerate 4 to 6 hours or overnight before serving.

Makes 16 Servings

Nutrients per Serving:
Calories 210 (Calories from Fat 110), Protein 7g, Fat 12g (Saturated Fat 7g), Carbohydrates 17g, Fiber 0g, Cholesterol 70mg, Sodium 210mg, Sugars 11g

Saucepan Rice Pudding

3 cups whole milk

¼ cup SPLENDA®
No Calorie Sweetener,
Granulated

2 teaspoons vanilla
extract

1 cinnamon stick

1 cup uncooked
long-grain rice

1 pinch salt

¼ cup raisins or mixed
dried fruit

2 tablespoons rum* or
orange juice

1 pinch nutmeg

*For dietary purposes, please
note that this recipe contains
alcohol.

1. Pour milk, SPLENDA® Granulated Sweetener, and vanilla into a medium saucepan. Add cinnamon stick. Bring to a boil. Add rice and salt. Cover and cook over low heat 30 minutes or until most of the milk is absorbed. Stir occasionally. Remove saucepan from heat. Set aside.

2. Place raisins (or mixed dried fruit) and rum (or orange juice) in small microwaveable bowl. Warm in a microwave briefly to plump the raisins. Add plumped raisins (or mixed fruit) to rice pudding.

3. Spoon into dessert dishes. Sprinkle with nutmeg. Serve warm or chilled.

Makes 5 Servings

Nutrients per Serving:
Calories 180 (Calories from Fat 45), Protein 6g, Fat 5g (Saturated Fat 3g),
Carbohydrates 25g, Fiber 1g, Cholesterol 20mg, Sodium 150mg, Sugars 12g

Sour Cream Apple Cobbler

Fruit Filling:

- ⅓ cup SPLENDA® No Calorie Sweetener, Granulated
- 2 tablespoons all-purpose flour
- ½ teaspoon ground cinnamon
- 1 cup unsweetened apple juice
- 1 tablespoon fresh lemon juice
- 1 teaspoon fresh grated lemon zest
- 1 tablespoon butter
- 6 medium Granny Smith apples, peeled and sliced
- ½ cup golden raisins (optional)

Topping:

- 1 cup all-purpose flour
- 2 tablespoons SPLENDA® No Calorie Sweetener, Granulated
- ½ teaspoon baking powder
- ½ teaspoon baking soda
- ¼ teaspoon salt
- 3 tablespoons cold butter, cut into small pieces
- ⅔ cup reduced-fat sour cream
- ¼ cup nonfat milk
- 1 teaspoon vanilla extract

1. Preheat oven to 375°F. Spray an 8-inch square baking dish with nonstick cooking spray; set aside.

2. Whisk together SPLENDA® Granulated Sweetener, flour, cinnamon, apple juice, lemon juice, and lemon zest in a medium bowl; set aside.

3. Melt butter in a large nonstick skillet over medium-high heat; add apples and cook, stirring often, until softened, 8 minutes. Stir in apple juice mixture and bring to a boil; stir in raisins, if desired. Spoon apple mixture into prepared baking dish.

4. **Prepare Topping:** Combine flour, SPLENDA® Granulated Sweetener, baking powder, baking soda, and salt in the bowl of a food processor; add butter and pulse until mixture resembles coarse meal. Transfer mixture to a medium bowl; stir in sour cream, milk, and vanilla. Drop dough by spoonfuls onto the apple mixture; bake in preheated oven 25 minutes or until Topping is lightly browned. Serve warm.

Makes 6 Servings

Nutrients per Serving:
Calories 320 (Calories from Fat 100), Protein 5g, Fat 11g (Saturated Fat 7g), Carbohydrates 55g, Fiber 4g, Cholesterol 30mg, Sodium 320mg, Sugars 30g

PREP TIME: **3 Minutes**
TOTAL TIME: **3 Hours, 3 Minutes**

Chocolate Yogurt Pops

- **1 (8-ounce) container plain nonfat yogurt**
- **¼ cup sugar-free cocoa mix**
- **¼ cup SPLENDA® No Calorie Sweetener, Granulated**
- **4 ice cream sticks**

1. Mix all ingredients in a small mixing bowl. Spoon mixture into 4 (3-ounce) paper cups. Set cups in a muffin pan or on a flat plate. Place ice cream sticks in the center. Freeze about 3 hours or until solid.
2. Peel paper cups away from popsicles before serving.

Makes 4 Servings

Nutrients per Serving:
Calories 50 (Calories from Fat 0), Protein 4g, Fat 0g (Saturated Fat 0g), Carbohydrates 10g, Fiber 0g, Cholesterol 0mg, Sodium 80mg, Sugars 8g

Boston Cream Pie

Cake:

- 1¾ **cups sifted cake flour**
- ½ **cup SPLENDA® Sugar Blend**
- 2 **teaspoons baking powder**
- ½ **teaspoon salt**
- ⅓ **cup butter, softened**
- 2 **large eggs, lightly beaten**
- ⅓ **cup 1% low-fat milk**
- 1 **teaspoon vanilla extract**

Custard:

- 1 **tablespoon SPLENDA® Sugar Blend**
- 1½ **tablespoons cornstarch**
- ⅛ **teaspoon salt**
- 1 **cup 1% low-fat milk**
- 2 **egg yolks, lightly beaten**
- ½ **teaspoon vanilla extract**

Glaze:

- 6 **tablespoons whipping cream**
- 4 **(1-ounce) squares semisweet chocolate, finely chopped**

1. **Prepare Cake:** Preheat oven to 350°F. Lightly grease and flour 2 (8-inch) cake pans. Set aside.

2. Combine flour, SPLENDA® Sugar Blend, baking powder, and salt in a large mixing bowl. Cut butter into flour mixture with a fork or a pastry blender until crumbly. (This procedure may be done with a mixer at the lowest speed. Cover mixing bowl with a clean tea towel to prevent spattering).

3. Combine eggs, milk, and vanilla in a small mixing bowl; add ⅓ of the egg mixture to flour mixture. Beat at low speed of an electric mixer until blended. Beat at medium speed for 30 seconds or until batter is smooth, stopping to scrape down sides of bowl. Repeat procedure 2 times.

4. Spoon batter evenly into prepared pans.

5. Bake in preheated oven 15 minutes or until a wooden pick inserted in centers comes out clean. Cool in pans on wire racks 10 minutes; remove from pans and cool on wire racks.

6. Spread Custard Filling between cake layers. Spread Chocolate Glaze over top.

Nutrients per Serving:
Calories 280 (Calories from Fat 120), Protein 5g, Fat 13g (Saturated Fat 7g), Carbohydrates 33g, Fiber 1g, Cholesterol 95mg, Sodium 280mg, Sugars 16g

Custard Directions: Combine SPLENDA® Sugar Blend, cornstarch, and salt in a heavy saucepan, mixing well. Gradually whisk milk into SPLENDA® Sugar Blend mixture. Cook over medium heat, whisking constantly until thickened and bubbly. Remove from heat.

Beat egg yolks until thick and pale. Gradually whisk ½ cup of hot custard mixture into yolks; return to remaining hot custard mixture, whisking constantly. Cook over medium heat for 1 minute or until mixture comes to a boil, whisking constantly. Remove from heat; stir in vanilla. Cover with plastic wrap, gently pressing on filling. Cool slightly.

Glaze Directions: Heat whipping cream in a small saucepan until cream is thoroughly warmed; stir in chocolate. Cook over low heat, stirring constantly, until chocolate melts.

Makes 12 Servings

Irresistible Lemon Chiffon Pie

1 **cup evaporated milk**

1 **(.25-ounce) envelope unflavored gelatin**

½ **cup water**

3 **tablespoons fresh lemon juice**

¾ **cup SPLENDA® No Calorie Sweetener, Granulated**

¾ **teaspoon grated lemon rind**

¼ **teaspoon lemon extract (optional)**

1 **(9-inch) graham cracker crust**

1. Pour evaporated milk in a mixing bowl; place in freezer until ice crystals form (about 30 minutes).

2. Sprinkle gelatin over water and lemon juice in a small saucepan; let stand 1 minute. Stir in SPLENDA® Granulated Sweetener and cook over medium heat, stirring constantly, 2 minutes or until gelatin dissolves. Stir in lemon rind and lemon extract, if desired.

3. Beat evaporated milk at high speed with an electric mixer until soft peaks form (about 5 minutes). Gradually add gelatin mixture, beating at high speed until mixture is combined. Do not overbeat.

4. Pour mixture into crust; cover and chill 1 hour or until set.

Makes 8 Servings

Nutrients per Serving:
Calories 200 (Calories from Fat 90), Protein 4g, Fat 10g (Saturated Fat 3g), Carbohydrates 25g, Fiber 0g, Cholesterol 10mg, Sodium 210mg, Sugars 16g

S'mores Campfire Pie

Filling:

- ½ **cup SPLENDA® Sugar Blend**
- ⅓ **cup fat-free half and half**
- 1 **teaspoon vanilla extract**
- 4 **(1-ounce) squares unsweetened chocolate, chopped**
- 1 **(9-inch) graham cracker crust**

Meringue:

- 4 **egg whites**
- ¼ **teaspoon cream of tartar**
- 1 **teaspoon vanilla extract**
- ½ **cup SPLENDA® Sugar Blend**

1. **Prepare Filling:** Combine SPLENDA® Sugar Blend and half and half in a small saucepan. Cook over medium heat, stirring constantly, until SPLENDA® Sugar Blend dissolves. Stir in vanilla; add chocolate, stirring until chocolate melts. Pour mixture into crust. Set aside.

2. Preheat oven to 225°F.

3. **Prepare Meringue:** Combine egg whites, cream of tartar, and vanilla in a large bowl; beat at high speed with an electric mixer until foamy. Gradually add SPLENDA® Sugar Blend, 1 tablespoon at a time, beating until stiff peaks form and SPLENDA® Sugar Blend dissolves. Spread meringue evenly over chocolate filling.

4. Bake in preheated oven 2 hours. Turn oven off and leave in oven, with door closed and oven light on for 8 hours or overnight.

Makes 8 Servings

Nutrients per Serving:
Calories 340 (Calories from Fat 130), Protein 5g, Fat 14g (Saturated Fat 6g), Carbohydrates 46g, Fiber 3g, Cholesterol 0mg, Sodium 190mg, Sugars 37g

Baked Apple Turnovers

4 Granny Smith apples, peeled and chopped

⅓ cup water

¼ cup SPLENDA® No Calorie Sweetener, Granulated

2 tablespoons all-purpose flour

¼ teaspoon ground cinnamon

1 (15-ounce) package refrigerated pie crusts

1 egg white, lightly beaten

1. Cook apples and water in a medium saucepan over medium heat, covered, stirring occasionally and breaking up apples with the back of a spoon, 10 to 12 minutes or until apples form a coarse purée. Add SPLENDA® Granulated Sweetener and flour; cook 2 to 3 additional minutes, stirring constantly until SPLENDA® Granulated Sweetener dissolves and mixture is thickened. Stir in cinnamon. Spoon apple mixture into a bowl to cool slightly.

2. Preheat oven to 425°F. Coat a baking sheet with nonstick cooking spray; set aside.

3. Unroll pie crusts; cut each one into 4 wedges. Roll each wedge into a 6-inch circle. Place 3 level tablespoons apple mixture on each circle; moisten edges of dough with water and fold dough over to form a half-moon shape. Crimp to seal, and cut vents to release steam. Place on prepared pan; brush tops with egg white.

4. Bake in preheated oven 15 to 20 minutes or until turnovers are browned. Cool turnovers on a wire rack 10 minutes before serving. Serve warm or at room temperature.

Makes 8 Servings

Nutrients per Serving:
Calories 290 (Calories from Fat 140), Protein 3g, Fat 16g (Saturated Fat 2g), Carbohydrates 34g, Fiber 2g, Cholesterol 0mg, Sodium 320mg, Sugars 8g

EZ Baked Apples

6 Granny Smith apples

**1 cup SPLENDA®
No Calorie Sweetener,
Granulated**

**1 teaspoon ground
cinnamon**

1 tablespoon margarine

1. Preheat oven to 350°F.

2. Wash apples and core using an apple corer. Place in a 9×13-inch baking pan.

3. Mix together SPLENDA® Granulated Sweetener and cinnamon. Fill each apple with the mixture and then top each apple with a small dot of margarine. Cover with aluminum foil and bake in preheated oven 45 to 50 minutes or until slightly soft.

Makes 6 Servings

Nutrients per Serving:
Calories 110 (Calories from Fat 20), Protein 0g, Fat 2g (Saturated Fat 0g),
Carbohydrates 25g, Fiber 4g, Cholesterol 0mg, Sodium 20mg, Sugars 20g

Delicious Smoothies
& Other Beverages

Splenda
Brand

Be sweet.
Pass it on.

Raspberry Whip

1 **stick SPLENDA®**
   No Calorie Sweetener
   FLAVOR ACCENTS™,
   Raspberry

¼ **cup sugar-free**
   nondairy whipped
   topping

   Small drop red food
   coloring

   Ice, as desired

½ **cup diet lemon-lime**
   soda

1. Mix SPLENDA® No Calorie Sweetener FLAVOR ACCENTS™ and nondairy whipped topping in a small bowl. Mix in food coloring.

2. Place ice in a tall clear glass. Pour diet lemon lime soda into glass filled with ice. Top with whipped topping mixture. Serve immediately.

Makes 1 Serving

Nutrients per Serving:
Calories 45 (Calories from Fat 20), Protein 0g, Fat 2g (Saturated Fat 2g), Carbohydrates 8g, Fiber 0g, Cholesterol 0mg, Sodium 20mg, Sugars 0g

Citrus Berry Spritzer

2 teaspoons raspberry or apple raspberry juice concentrate

1 stick SPLENDA® No Calorie Sweetener FLAVOR ACCENTS™, Lemon

1 stick SPLENDA® No Calorie Sweetener FLAVOR ACCENTS™, Raspberry

½ cup seltzer or sparkling mineral water

½ cup orange juice

Ice, as desired

1. Thaw raspberry juice concentrate. Set aside.
2. Mix SPLENDA® No Calorie Sweetener FLAVOR ACCENTS™ into seltzer water. Add orange juice.
3. Place ice in a tall clear glass. Pour juice mixture into glass. Spoon juice concentrate on top. Serve immediately.

Makes 1 Serving

Nutrients per Serving:
Calories 80 (Calories from Fat 0), Protein 1g, Fat 0g (Saturated Fat 0g), Carbohydrates 21g, Fiber 2g, Cholesterol 0mg, Sodium 40mg, Sugars 17g

Café con Leche

2 (1¼-fluid-ounce) shots espresso

1½ cups 2% reduced-fat milk

1 cinnamon stick

2 tablespoons SPLENDA® Brown Sugar Blend

Add all ingredients to a small pot. Heat over medium heat until hot.

Makes 2 Servings

Nutrients per Serving:
Calories 140 (Calories from Fat 30), Protein 6g, Fat 3.5g (Saturated Fat 2g), Carbohydrates 21g, Fiber 0g, Cholesterol 15mg, Sodium 75mg, Sugars 20g

Berry-Banana Smoothie

2 cups 1% low-fat milk

1 ripe banana, sliced

½ cup SPLENDA® No Calorie Sweetener, Granulated

1 (0.13-ounce) package KOOL-AID® Strawberry Flavor Unsweetened Soft Drink Mix

2 cups ice cubes

Process milk, banana, SPLENDA® Granulated Sweetener, KOOL-AID® Soft Drink Mix, and ice cubes in a blender until smooth, stopping to scrape down sides. Serve immediately.

Makes 4 Servings

Nutrients per Serving:
Calories 80 (Calories from Fat 15), Protein 4g, Fat 1g (Saturated Fat 1g), Carbohydrates 13g, Fiber 1g, Cholesterol 5mg, Sodium 110mg, Sugars 11g

Banana Strawberry Shake

1 **large ripe banana,
sliced**

5 **packets SPLENDA®
No Calorie Sweetener**

½ **cup 2% reduced-fat
milk**

1¼ **cups frozen
unsweetened
strawberries**

1. Combine all ingredients in a blender. Blend on medium speed until smooth.

2. Pour into glasses and serve.

Makes 2 Servings

Nutrients per Serving:
Calories 140 (Calories from Fat 15), Protein 3g, Fat 2g (Saturated Fat 1g),
Carbohydrates 31g, Fiber 5g, Cholesterol 5mg, Sodium 35mg, Sugars 25g

Soothing Warm Milk

2 cups 1% low-fat milk

2 teaspoons vanilla extract

1 tablespoon SPLENDA® No Calorie Sweetener, Granulated

½ teaspoon ground nutmeg

In 2 large mugs, stir together the milk, vanilla, and SPLENDA® Granulated Sweetener. Heat in the microwave on full power for 2 minutes. Stir in nutmeg and serve hot.

Makes 2 Servings

Nutrients per Serving:
Calories 120 (Calories from Fat 25), Protein 9g, Fat 3g (Saturated Fat 2g), Carbohydrates 13g, Fiber 0g, Cholesterol 10mg, Sodium 130mg, Sugars 0g

Lemon Lime KOOL-AID® Milk Shake

1 **pint no-sugar-added
light vanilla ice cream**

1 **cup 1% low-fat milk**

¼ **cup SPLENDA®
No Calorie Sweetener,
Granulated**

1 **(0.13 ounce)
package KOOL-AID®
Unsweetened
Lemon-Lime Flavored
Drink Mix**

Process ice cream, milk, SPLENDA® Granulated
Sweetener, and KOOL-AID® Soft Drink Mix in
a blender until smooth, stopping to scrape
down sides. Serve immediately.

Makes 3 Servings

Nutrients per Serving:
Calories 190 (Calories from Fat 60), Protein 7g, Fat 7g (Saturated Fat 4g),
Carbohydrates 24g, Fiber 0g, Cholesterol 20mg, Sodium 140mg, Sugars 14g

Mock Sangria

2 **sticks SPLENDA®**
   No Calorie Sweetener
   FLAVOR ACCENTS™,
   Lemon

1 **thin slice fresh lemon**

2 **thin slices fresh orange**

1 **cup alcohol-removed**
   wine

3 **thin slices fresh apple**

   Ice, as desired

Crush SPLENDA® No Calorie Sweetener FLAVOR ACCENTS™, lemon and orange slices with a fork in a tall glass. Add wine and stir. Add apple slices and ice as desired. Serve immediately.

Makes 1 Serving

Hot Tea Punch

3 packets SPLENDA®
  No Calorie Sweetener

1 (3-inch) cinnamon stick

1 whole clove

1 cup water

2 tea bags

½ cup fresh orange juice

2 teaspoons fresh lemon
  juice

1. Bring SPLENDA® Granulated Sweetener, cinnamon stick, clove, and water to a boil in a heavy saucepan; boil 2 minutes. Remove from heat and add tea bags. Cover and steep for 5 minutes. Remove spices and tea bags with a slotted spoon.

2. Stir in juices. Serve immediately.

Makes 2 Servings

Nutrients per Serving:
Calories 35 (Calories from Fat 0), Protein 1g, Fat 0g (Saturated Fat 0g),
Carbohydrates 9g, Fiber 1g, Cholesterol 0mg, Sodium 5mg, Sugars 7g

Caramel Latte

**2 sticks SPLENDA®
Flavors for Coffee,
Caramel**

¼ **cup brewed espresso**

¼ **teaspoon vanilla
extract**

½ **cup 2% reduced-fat
milk**

1. Mix all ingredients together in a microwaveable bowl or mug. Heat in microwave 30 to 40 seconds or to desired temperature.

2. Blend in blender 15 to 20 seconds to create a frothy drink, if desired. Pour into serving cup and serve immediately.

Makes 1 Serving

Nutrients per Serving:
Calories 70 (Calories from Fat 20), Protein 4g, Fat 2g (Saturated Fat 2g),
Carbohydrates 9g, Fiber 0g, Cholesterol 10mg, Sodium 70mg, Sugars 6g

Triple Grape KOOL-AID® Brain Freeze

- **2 cups ice cubes**
- **½ cup SPLENDA® No Calorie Sweetener, Granulated**
- **2 (.13-ounce) envelopes KOOL-AID® Grape Flavor Unsweetened Soft Drink Mix**
- **2 cups red seedless grapes, frozen***
- **1½ cups unsweetened purple grape juice**

To freeze grapes, individually remove them from the stems, wash thoroughly, and blot dry. Place in zip-top plastic bags and freeze to have ready whenever you need them.

Combine all ingredients in a blender in the order listed; process mixture until smooth, stopping to scrape down sides.

Makes 4 Servings

Nutrients per Serving:
Calories 120 (Calories from Fat 5), Protein 1g, Fat 1g (Saturated Fat 0g),
Carbohydrates 28g, Fiber 1g, Cholesterol 0mg, Sodium 45mg, Sugars 28g

Blackberry Twist Lemonade

**2 cups fresh blackberries,
or unsweetened
frozen blackberries,
thawed**

1 cup fresh lemon juice

**1 cup SPLENDA®
No Calorie Sweetener,
Granulated**

4 cups cold water

Combine blackberries, lemon juice, and
SPLENDA® Granulated Sweetener in a blender;
process until smooth, stopping to scrape
down sides. Press mixture through a sieve into
a pitcher; discard solids. Stir in water. Serve
over ice.

Makes 7 Servings

Nutrients per Serving:
Calories 30 (Calories from Fat 0), Protein 0g, Fat 0g (Saturated Fat 0g),
Carbohydrates 8g, Fiber 2g, Cholesterol 0mg, Sodium 0mg, Sugars 4g

Banana Punch Slush

4 **ripe bananas**

¾ **cup SPLENDA®
No Calorie Sweetener,
Granulated**

6 **cups water, divided**

1 **(46-fluid-ounce) can
pineapple juice**

2 **(12-fluid-ounce) cans
frozen orange juice
concentrate**

1 **(12-fluid-ounce) can
frozen lemonade
concentrate**

3 **liters ginger ale**

1. In a blender, combine bananas, SPLENDA® Granulated Sweetener, and 3 cups water. Blend until smooth. Pour into a large bowl and stir in pineapple juice. Stir in orange juice concentrate, lemonade concentrate, and 3 more cups water. Divide into 3 plastic containers and freeze until solid.

2. Remove from freezer 3 to 4 hours before serving. Using 1 portion at a time, place slush in a punch bowl and pour in 1 liter of ginger ale for each.

Makes 54 Servings

Nutrients per Serving:
Calories 80 (Calories from Fat 0), Protein 0g, Fat 0g (Saturated Fat 0g),
Carbohydrates 19g, Fiber 0g, Cholesterol 0mg, Sodium 10mg, Sugars 18g

Grapefruit Raspberry Sparkler

1 cup fresh raspberries or unsweetened frozen raspberries, thawed

1¼ cups grapefruit juice

3 tablespoons SPLENDA® No Calorie Sweetener, Granulated

1⅓ cups diet lemon-lime soda

1. Process raspberries, grapefruit juice, and SPLENDA® Granulated Sweetener in a blender until smooth. Press mixture through a sieve into a pitcher; discard solids.

2. Fill 4 tall glasses with ice and pour about ½ cup of the raspberry mixture into each one. Add ⅓ cup of the soda to each glass. Serve immediately.

Makes 4 Servings

Nutrients per Serving:
Calories 50 (Calories from Fat 0), Protein 1g, Fat 0g (Saturated Fat 0g), Carbohydrates 12g, Fiber 2g, Cholesterol 0mg, Sodium 10mg, Sugars 9g

Raspberry Hot Chocolate

2 sticks SPLENDA®
No Calorie Sweetener
FLAVOR ACCENTS™,
Raspberry

1 packet sugar-free hot
cocoa mix

1 cup 1% low-fat milk

1. Mix SPLENDA® No Calorie Sweetener FLAVOR ACCENTS™ and dry cocoa mix together in a mug or coffee cup. Heat milk on stovetop or in microwave.

2. Pour hot milk into mug. Stir well. Serve immediately.

Makes 1 Serving

Nutrients per Serving:
Calories 150 (Calories from Fat 25), Protein 12g, Fat 3g (Saturated Fat 2g),
Carbohydrates 22g, Fiber 0g, Cholesterol 10mg, Sodium 220mg, Sugars 19g

Banana Colada Smoothie

1 **cup ice cubes**

1 **cup chopped fresh pineapple**

1 **small ripe banana, sliced**

3 **tablespoons SPLENDA® No Calorie Sweetener, Granulated**

½ **cup reduced-fat coconut milk**

½ **teaspoon vanilla extract**

Combine all ingredients in a blender in the order listed; process mixture until smooth, stopping to scrape down sides.

Makes 2 Servings

Nutrients per Serving:
Calories 140 (Calories from Fat 50), Protein 1g, Fat 6g (Saturated Fat 3g),
Carbohydrates 23g, Fiber 2g, Cholesterol 0mg, Sodium 10mg, Sugars 18g

Horchata

3 **sticks SPLENDA®
Flavors for Coffee,
Cinnamon Spice**

¾ **cup low-fat almond
milk**

⅛ **teaspoon fresh lime
juice**

Ice, as desired

Stir ingredients together in a tall glass. Add
ice. Serve immediately.

Makes 1 Serving

Nutrients per Serving:
Calories 45 (Calories from Fat 20), Protein 1g, Fat 2g (Saturated Fat 0g),
Carbohydrates 9g, Fiber 1g, Cholesterol 0mg, Sodium 120mg, Sugars 5g

Atole

¼ **cup masa flour**

½ **cups water***

½ **tablespoons SPLENDA®
   Brown Sugar Blend**

1 **teaspoon molasses**

½ **vanilla bean, split
   lengthwise**

1 **cinnamon stick**

*ilk can be used in place
water to create a thicker
verage.*

Add all ingredients to a medium saucepan. Heat over medium heat. Whisk until mixture begins to thicken. Remove cinnamon stick and vanilla bean. Serve hot or warm. Garnish with additional cinnamon sticks, if desired.

Strawberry variation: Stir in 1 cup puréed strawberries just before serving.

Makes 3 Servings

trients per Serving:
ories 80 (Calories from Fat 0), Protein 1g, Fat 0g (Saturated Fat 0g),
bohydrate 20g, Fiber 1g, Cholesterol 0mg, Sodium 5mg, Sugars 11g

Hot White Chocolate

1 **stick SPLENDA® Flavors for Coffee, French Vanilla**

2 **tablespoons white chocolate chips**

½ **cup skim milk**

½ **cup fat-free half and half**

Place ingredients into large mug. Microwave until hot, stirring every 30 seconds.

Makes 1 Serving

Nutrients per Serving:
Calories 240 (Calories from Fat 70), Protein 9g, Fat 7g (Saturated Fat 5g), Carbohydrates 32g, Fiber 0g, Cholesterol 25mg, Sodium 200mg, Sugars 27g

Caramel Apple Cider

1 **stick SPLENDA®
No Calorie Sweetener
Flavors for Coffee,
Caramel**

2 **sticks SPLENDA®
No Calorie Sweetener
Flavors for Coffee,
Cinnamon Spice**

1 **cup apple cider or
apple juice**

Mix all ingredients together in a large mug or coffee cup. Heat in microwave until warm. Serve immediately.

Makes 1 Serving

Nutrients per Serving:
Calories 120 (Calories from Fat 0), Protein 0g, Fat 0g (Saturated Fat 0g),
Carbohydrates 32g, Fiber 0g, Cholesterol 0mg, Sodium 25mg, Sugars 26g

Cherry Vanilla KOOL-AID® Malt

2½ **cups no-sugar-added light vanilla ice cream**

⅓ **cup malted milk powder**

¼ **cup SPLENDA® No Calorie Sweetener, Granulated**

1 **(0.13-ounce) package KOOL-AID® Cherry Flavor Unsweetened Soft Drink Mix**

1½ **cups 2% reduced-fat milk**

Light whipped topping (optional)

Fresh cherries (optional)

1. Combine all ingredients in a blender in the order listed; process mixture until smooth, stopping to scrape down sides.

2. Garnish with light whipped topping and a fresh cherry, if desired.

Makes 4 Servings

Nutrients per Serving:
Calories 260 (Calories from Fat 70), Protein 9g, Fat 8g (Saturated Fat 5g), Carbohydrates 38g, Fiber 0g, Cholesterol 25mg, Sodium 230mg, Sugars 21g

Virgin Mojito

- **6 mint leaves**
- **1 tablespoon SPLENDA® No Calorie Sweetener, Granulated**
- **1 lime, juiced**
- **1 (12-ounce) can diet lemon-lime soda, chilled**
- **Fresh mint for garnish (optional)**
- **Lime slices for garnish (optional)**

1. Smash mint leafs and SPLENDA® Granulated Sweetener with a spoon in the bottom of a large glass.
2. Add lime juice and stir. Pour in soda and stir well.* Garnish with mint and lime slice. Serve chilled.

---

*A cocktail shaker can be used to create a frothier beverage. Add ice and mojito to a shaker and shake well.

Makes 1 Serving

Nutrients per Serving:
Calories 20 (Calories from Fat 0), Protein 0g, Fat 0g (Saturated Fat 0g), Carbohydrates 6g, Fiber 0g, Cholesterol 0mg, Sodium 55mg, Sugars 3g

PREP TIME: **2 Minutes**
TOTAL TIME: **2 Minutes**

Mulled Cranberry 'Cider'

- **5 sticks SPLENDA® Flavors for Coffee, Cinnamon Spice**
- **¾ cup brewed chai tea**
- **¾ cup apple juice**
- **1½ cups cranberry juice**

Mix all ingredients together. Heat in a saucepan on the stovetop 1 to 2 minutes or in microwave to desired temperature. Pour into mugs. Serve immediately.

Makes 3 Servings

Splenda Brand

Nutrients per Serving:
Calories 100 (Calories from Fat 0), Protein 0g, Fat 0g (Saturated Fat 0g), Carbohydrates 27g, Fiber 0g, Cholesterol 0mg, Sodium 5mg, Sugars 25g

Mexican Hot Chocolate with Cayenne Pepper and Orange Zest

¼ **cup water**

6 **tablespoons unsweetened cocoa powder**

¼ **cup SPLENDA® No Calorie Sweetener, Granulated**

1 **tablespoon vanilla extract**

1 **tablespoon grated orange peel**

½ **teaspoon cayenne pepper**

5½ **cups nonfat milk**

2 **cinnamon sticks**

⅛ **teaspoon salt**

1. Whisk water, cocoa powder, and SPLENDA® Granulated Sweetener in a saucepan. Slowly bring to a simmer over medium heat, stirring constantly. Cook until mixture thickens and resembles a syrup.

2. Mix in remaining ingredients and heat. Do not boil. Serve hot.

Makes 6 Servings

Nutrients per Serving:
Calories 110 (Calories from Fat 10), Protein 9g, Fat 1g (Saturated Fat 1g), Carbohydrates 16g, Fiber 3g, Cholesterol 5mg, Sodium 170mg, Sugars 12g

Breakfast

Cookies & Bars

Splenda

VOLUME MEASUREMENTS (dry)

1/8 teaspoon = 0.5 mL
1/4 teaspoon = 1 mL
1/2 teaspoon = 2 mL
3/4 teaspoon = 4 mL
1 teaspoon = 5 mL
1 tablespoon = 15 mL
2 tablespoons = 30 mL
1/4 cup = 60 mL
1/3 cup = 75 mL
1/2 cup = 125 mL
2/3 cup = 150 mL
3/4 cup = 175 mL
1 cup = 250 mL
2 cups = 1 pint = 500 mL
3 cups = 750 mL
4 cups = 1 quart = 1 L

VOLUME MEASUREMENTS (fluid)

1 fluid ounce (2 tablespoons) = 30 mL
4 fluid ounces (1/2 cup) = 125 mL
8 fluid ounces (1 cup) = 250 mL
12 fluid ounces (1 1/2 cups) = 375 mL
16 fluid ounces (2 cups) = 500 mL

WEIGHTS (mass)

1/2 ounce = 15 g
1 ounce = 30 g
3 ounces = 90 g
4 ounces = 120 g
8 ounces = 225 g
10 ounces = 285 g
12 ounces = 360 g
16 ounces = 1 pound = 450 g

DIMENSIONS

1/16 inch = 2 mm
1/8 inch = 3 mm
1/4 inch = 6 mm
1/2 inch = 1.5 cm
3/4 inch = 2 cm
1 inch = 2.5 cm

OVEN TEMPERATURES

250°F = 120°C
275°F = 140°C
300°F = 150°C
325°F = 160°C
350°F = 180°C
375°F = 190°C
400°F = 200°C
425°F = 220°C
450°F = 230°C

BAKING PAN SIZES

Utensil	Size in Inches/Quarts	Metric Volume	Size in Centimeters
Baking or Cake Pan (square or rectangular)	8×8×2	2 L	20×20×5
	9×9×2	2.5 L	23×23×5
	12×8×2	3 L	30×20×5
	13×9×2	3.5 L	33×23×5
Loaf Pan	8×4×3	1.5 L	20×10×7
	9×5×3	2 L	23×13×7
Round Layer Cake Pan	8×1½	1.2 L	20×4
	9×1½	1.5 L	23×4
Pie Plate	8×1¼	750 mL	20×3
	9×1¼	1 L	23×3
Baking Dish or Casserole	1 quart	1 L	—
	1½ quarts	1.5 L	—
	2 quarts	2 L	—